Editor
Walter Kelly, M.A.

Managing Editor
Karen Goldfluss, M.S. Ed.

Editor-in-Chief
Sharon Coan, M.S. Ed.

Illustrator
Ken Tunell

Cover Artist
Barb Lorseyedi

Art Coordinator
Kevin Barnes

Art Director
CJae Froshay

Imaging
Rosa C. See

Product Manager
Phil Garcia

Publishers
Rachelle Cracchiolo, M.S. Ed.
Mary Dupuy Smith, M.S. Ed.

Grades 4–6

Reading Skills Mini-Lessons

Rowe

Cause and Effect · Main Idea · Sequence · Context Clues · Prediction · Inference · Fact and Opinion · Setting

Author

Sara Gruver

Teacher Created Materials, Inc.
6421 Industry Way
Westminster, CA 92683
www.teachercreated.com

ISBN-0-7439-3288-9

©2003 Teacher Created Materials, Inc.

Reprinted, 2004

Made in U.S.A.

Table of Contents

Introduction

Why Mini-Lessons?

Mini-lessons are a great way to present focused reading lessons that concentrate on only one skill or strategy at a time. Mini-lessons differ from traditional reading lessons because of (1) their length and (2) their simplicity. The brief (10–20 minute) nature of mini-lessons successfully matches the attention span of intermediate students. The simple nature of mini-lessons helps students to feel successful by focusing on and mastering only one skill or strategy at a time. The brevity and simplicity of mini-lessons also allows for periodic review and practice of each skill and strategy taught.

Where Do Mini-Lessons Fit?

The versatility of mini-lessons allows them to be used to enhance any curriculum with any class schedule. Mini-lessons can be used to introduce a skill or strategy prior to reading workshop or silent reading time. They can be used as part of a read-aloud time to help students become more active during that time. They can also be used as part of small-group instruction for heterogeneous or homogeneous reading groups. Finally, mini-lessons can be used as quick daily reviews for state tests. Mini-lessons can serve a variety of needs and settings, but the purpose of mini-lessons remains the same: to present brief, focused lessons to improve students' reading.

Contents of This Book

This book presents a variety of short reading lessons, each focusing on one skill or strategy of importance for intermediate grade readers. The following are specific elements:

1. Each lesson contains a complete lesson plan, including an objective, materials list, suggested time frame, appropriate answer keys, and step-by-step procedures.

2. Many lesson plans also include "More Practice" suggestions with ideas for further practicing the skill in reading, as well as other curricular areas.

3. Some lesson plans also contain "Literature Connection" ideas for further practicing the skill or strategy with appropriate literature books. "Literature Connection" reproducible student activity sheets can be found at the back of this book.

4. Each skill and strategy includes a "Silent Reading Practice" reproducible sheet that provides a way for students to continue practicing the skill or strategy during their silent reading times. "Silent Reading Practice" sheets are in the back of the book.

5. Each lesson also contains a focused, reproducible student activity sheet that helps students to practice the skill or strategy they have just discussed. Student activity sheets include clear directions and a variety of activities.

Mini-Lesson #1: Context Clues

Teacher Lesson Plan

Objective

Students will explain what it means to use *context clues*. Students will practice using context clues to figure out the meaning of unknown words.

Summary

In this mini-lesson the teacher will use a game and discussion to introduce the strategy of using context clues to figure out the meaning of an unknown word. Students will practice using context clues to figure out the meaning of French words used on their student activity sheet.

Materials

- An overhead transparency of "What's Covered?" (*optional—see lesson plan below*)
- "Context Clues Practice" student activity sheet (1 copy per student, page 6)
- chalkboard or chart paper and markers

Time: 20 minutes

Lesson

Before the lesson: *Create an overhead transparency of "What's Covered?" (page 5) or copy the sentences onto the chalkboard or chart paper. Cover the underlined words.*

1. Introduction: Tell students that for today's game we are going to pretend that the covered word in each sentence is a word that we do not know. Display the "What's Covered?" overhead transparency or chart paper poster. Show students the first sentence and allow them to guess what the hidden word is. As students guess, ask them what made them think that. (*Students should begin to realize that they guessed those words because they would make sense.*) After an adequate number of students have guessed, reveal the covered word. Continue with other sentences in similar fashion.

2. Ask students how they were able to figure out the covered words. (*Thinking about the words around the covered word—thinking about what would make sense.*) Show students the definition of context clues on the "What's Covered?" activity and explain to students that they were using context clues to figure out what the covered words were. Tell students that context clues help us to figure out unknown words when we are reading.

3. Write the French words *corbeille*, *brosser*, *oublier*, *coq*, and *lentement* on the chalkboard or chart paper and ask students to guess their meanings. Tell students that these are French words and explain to them that it is difficult to figure out unknown words without any context to give you clues. Tell students that now you will give them these French words used within English sentences so that they will have context clues to help them figure out the meaning of the words.

4. Distribute the "Context Clues Practice" page to students and read the directions together. Allow students to complete the activity together and then review the answers. *See answer key below.*

Answer Key (page 6)		
1. trash can	3. forget	5. slowly
2. brush	4. rooster	

What's Covered?

The dog ran to fetch the <u>stick</u>.

The customers <u>complained</u> about the product because they were so dissatisfied.

I thought camp food would be gross, but actually I found it to be quite <u>delicious</u>.

"Come to the kitchen at <u>once</u>," shouted his brother.

It was so cold in the room that I put on my coat, <u>hat</u>, and gloves.

Look how <u>tiny</u> that dog is! I think that's the smallest dog I've ever seen!

The crowd <u>cheered</u> as their favorite team entered the field.

They <u>wasted</u> a lot of their time playing when they should have been working.

Context Clues

• Context clues are words or sentences around unknown words.

• Context clues help us figure out unknown words because they help us to realize what would make sense in the sentence.

Name _____   **Date** _____

Context Clues Practice

Directions: The underlined words in the following sentences are French words. Use the context clues to figure out the meaning of each word. Write the meaning in the blank.

---

1. That pen is broken. Throw it in the <u>corbeille</u>.

   Corbeille means _____.

---

2. The dentist told me I had a cavity. He tells me I must <u>brosser</u> my teeth at least twice a day.

   Brosser means _____.

---

3. Write this down because I do not want you to <u>oublier</u> it.

   Oublier means _____.

---

4. My grandma lives on a farm and has lots of farm animals. When I spend the night with her I am always awakened by the <u>coq</u> early in the morning.

   Coq means _____.

---

5. She cleaned up her room so <u>lentement</u> that I thought it would take her all day to get the job done.

   Lentement means_____.

Mini-Lesson #2: Context Clues

Teacher Lesson Plan

Objective

Students will identify why using context clues is a good way to figure out unknown words. Students will practice using context clues to figure out the meaning of words within sentences.

Summary

In this mini-lesson the students will brainstorm different ways to figure out unknown words in their reading. Then they will identify reasons why using context clues is a very good reading strategy. Finally students will practice using context clues once again on a student activity sheet.

Materials

- "More Context Clues Practice" student activity sheet (1 copy per student, pages 8, 9)
- chalkboard or overhead projector

Time: 20 minutes

Lesson

1. Introduction: Ask students what they do when they come to a word that they do not know while reading. Make a list on the chalkboard or overhead together. Ask students which strategy they think is the best. (*Guide students to see how using context clues is one of the best ways to figure out an unknown word.*)

2. Make a list together of reasons why using context clues is an excellent strategy. (*You can use this strategy when no one else is around; it might be quicker; it is a strategy you will use your whole life; it helps you to understand the text better; it helps you to remember the word better if you figure it out yourself; you do not have to put down your book and go look it up; you do not have to take time to look it up in a dictionary and figure out which definition is the correct one.*)

3. Distribute "More Context Clues Practice" student activity sheets and read the directions together. Encourage students to test their friends and family at home to see if they can figure out the meanings of these words. *See the answer key below.*

More Practice

For more practice with context clues, ask students to create their own "What's Covered?" sentences (*as were used in Context Clues Mini-Lesson #1*). Students can then try out their sentences with their peers. If peers are unable to guess the covered word, encourage students to revise their sentences with more precise context clues. You may want to try this activity with new vocabulary words as well.

Answer Key (pages 8 and 9)

1. odd, remarkable	5. hard to please
2. a cut made by a saw	6. one who gives unwanted advice
3. useless ornament or accessory	7. rejoiced, showed joy
4. cow	

Name_____   **Date** _____

More Context Clues Practice

Directions: The **boldface underlined** words in the following sentences are unusual words. Use the context clues to figure out the meaning of each word. Write a sentence to explain what you think each underlined word means.

1. This is so **phenomenal!** I can't believe this mountain! I've never seen anything like it before!

_____

_____

2. Who made that **kerf** in the log? Whoever did it must have used a pretty big saw to make a cut that deep.

_____

_____

3. Elsa refused to wear flowers in her hair for her wedding because she insisted that they were **folderol**. Elsa felt that the flowers made her look silly and that they were unnecessary.

_____

_____

More Context Clues Practice *(cont.)*

Directions: The **boldface underlined** words in the following sentences are unusual words. Use the context clues to figure out the meaning of each word. Write a sentence to explain what you think each underlined word means.

4. Have you ever been to a farm where they have **kine**? The farm I went to was a milking farm so they didn't use the **kine** for meat.

_____

_____

5. My coach is so **fastidious**. It seems like no matter how hard we work she's not pleased.

_____

_____

6. I think I would have enjoyed the card game much more if my big sister had not been such a **kibitzer**. I got very tired of her hanging over my shoulder to give me tips.

_____

_____

7. After Attila's team won the championship, they **jubilated** together. The coach bought the team ice cream and they congratulated each other all evening.

_____

_____

Mini-Lesson #3: Context Clues

Teacher Lesson Plan

Objective

Students will identify why using context clues is a good way to figure out unknown words. Students will practice using context clues to figure out the meaning of words within sentences.

Summary

In this mini-lesson the teacher will lead students in a brief discussion of context clues, and then students will be asked to complete a student activity sheet that requires them to use and reflect upon their use of context clues.

Materials

- "Context Clues Masters" activity sheet (1 copy per student, page 11)
- "More Context Clues Practice" activity sheet (1 copy per student, page 12)

Time: 20 minutes

Lesson

1. Introduction: Ask students how they would define "context clues." Ask students to share the different ways that the class has used context clues in the mini-lessons so far. Ask students to think again about why using context clues is a fine way to figure out unknown words. Tell students that they will once again need to use and think about context clues for today's activity.

2. Invite students to share examples of times they have used context clues other than when reading the mini-lessons.

3. Distribute "Context Clues Masters" and "More Context Clues Practice" student activity sheets and read the directions together. Allow students to complete activity sheets independently. Review students' answers to questions 1, 2, and 3 as time permits. *See the answer key below.*

More Practice

1. To demonstrate to students how useful context clues are, share an example of a time when you have recently used context clues to help you figure out an unknown word in a book or article. Also continue to emphasize the use of context clues by asking students to use context clues to figure out vocabulary words in curricular textbooks.

2. To continue an emphasis on the use of context clues, create a bulletin board entitled "Context Clues Masters." Invite students to copy down sentences from passages of writing that involve an unknown word that they figured out with the use of context clues. Attach students' examples on the board and encourage them to continue being context clues masters.

Silent Reading Practice

Refer to page 81 for a corresponding reproducible student sheet and directions.

Answer Key (page 11)		
1. small amount, crumb	2. weakened	3. downward slope

Name_____   **Date** _____

Context Clues Masters

Directions: The **boldface underlined** words in the following sentences are unusual words. Use the context clues to figure out the meaning of each word. Write a sentence to explain what you think each underlined word means.

1. I was hoping to be able to try a piece of that new cake, but by the time I got to it there was not one **iota** left of it.

_____

_____

2. We worked very hard all day to get the house painted, and by the end of the day we were so **enervated** that we had no strength left to do anything else.

_____

_____

3. It was difficult bicycling up the hill, but once we started back down the **declivity**, we really picked up speed.

_____

_____

Name_____   **Date** _____

More Context Clues Practice

Directions: Answer the following questions.

1. List at least four things that you can do when you are reading a book and come to a word that you do not know:

   _____

   _____

   _____

   _____

   _____

   _____

2. How would you define "context clues"?

   _____

   _____

   _____

3. What do you think is the best thing to do when you are reading a book and come to a word that you do not know? How is this method better than other ways?

   _____

   _____

   _____

   _____

   _____

Mini-Lesson #4: Sequence

Teacher Lesson Plan

Objective

Students will define *sequence* and *flashback*. Students will sequence the events of a short story.

Summary

In this mini-lesson the teacher will lead students in a discussion of what a *sequence* is and help students to understand the meaning and purpose of a *flashback*. Then the teacher will guide the class to collectively complete one sequence activity. Finally the students will complete one sequence activity independently.

Materials

- overhead transparency or copies of "B-Ball" (page 14)
- "Medical School" and "Medical School, Version Two" activity sheets (1 per student, pages 15 and 16)

Time: 20 minutes

Lesson

1. Introduction: Write the word "sequence" on the board and invite students to share their definitions of "sequence." Guide students to understand how "sequence" relates to stories. Decide on a definition similar to *"the chronological order of the events that take place"* and write it on the board.

2. Ask students what a "flashback" is. Guide students towards a definition similar to *"a scene or event from the past that is inserted into a story"* and write it on the board. If applicable, share a familiar movie or book that utilizes flashbacks.

3. Ask students how a flashback affects the sequence of a story. Tell students that oftentimes flashbacks often confuse young readers about the sequence of events in a story. Tell students that today we will practice putting events of a story in their proper sequence. Remind students that the sequence of a story is the actual order that the events happened and *not* necessarily the order that the author writes the events. Tell students that you want them to pay special attention to the flashbacks in the stories that they read today.

4. Display overhead or distribute copies of "B-Ball." Read the story and complete the sequence activity together. *See the answer key below.*

5. Ask students if they have ever thought about going to medical school. Tell students to pay close attention to flashbacks used in this story about a young man who went to medical school. Distribute copies of "Medical School" and "Medical School, Version Two." Review directions and allow students to complete the activities independently. *See the answer key below.*

6. When students have completed the activities, discuss how the two versions of the "Medical School" story were different. (*The second version did not use flashbacks.*)

Answer Key (pages 14 and 15)

(page 14—"B-Ball" 4, 1, 3, 6, 2, 5) and (page 15—"Medical School" 7, 4, 2, 6, 1, 5, 3)

Name_____   Date _____

B-Ball

Directions: Read the following story and then number the events in the order in which they occurred.

Eddie has always been into sports. Before playing basketball, he played soccer. His soccer team went to the state championships and won a trophy when he was in the fifth grade. It was a very exciting game, and Eddie scored the winning goal!

Now Eddie plays basketball on the ninth grade basketball team. Next year he will try out for the 10th grade soccer team as well. Then he will be playing team sports practically all year round. When Eddie was five years old, his big sister took him to a college soccer game and that's when he decided that he wanted to play on a sports team.

Today, his sister Jessica comes to his basketball games and claims that she inspired him to be the great athlete that he is. Eddie just laughs when she says that, but he does agree that she had a part in his love for athletics. Jessica frequently tells him that if he works hard he can do anything. Eddie's most recent dream is to go to college on a basketball scholarship and study physics.

_____ Eddie plays on the ninth grade basketball team.

_____ Eddie decides that he wants to play on a sports team.

_____ Eddie's fifth grade soccer team won the state championships.

_____ Eddie hopes to go to college and study physics.

_____ Eddie scored the winning goal on his fifth grade soccer team.

_____ Eddie will try out for the 10th grade soccer team.

Name _____

Date _____

6

Medical School

Directions: Read the following story and then number the events in the order in which they happened.

This is Aaron's third year in medical school. He began medical school at University School of Medicine after he graduated from Mount Vernon College. Now he is both working in a lab and taking classes.

When Aaron was in the eighth grade, he visited a doctor on Career Day and learned that being a doctor was a great way to help people. Aaron decided that he wanted to be a doctor some day. He pursued his dream by going to college.

At Mount Vernon College Aaron took a lot of chemistry and biology classes. Some of these classes were review, though, because Aaron had also taken chemistry and biology courses in high school. Also, while in high school Aaron volunteered at the hospital, and these experiences helped him in college as well. Aaron worked very hard through college and earned good grades.

Although he is in his third year of medical school, Aaron has not yet decided what type of doctor he would like to be. Aaron enjoys research and may decide to use his medical degree to do research or teach. Aaron is glad that he decided to attend medical school.

_____ Aaron is working in a lab and taking classes.

_____ Aaron took a lot of chemistry and biology classes at Mount Vernon College.

_____ Aaron volunteered at the hospital.

_____ Aaron is in his third year of medical school.

_____ Aaron decided in the eighth grade that he wanted to be a doctor.

_____ Aaron began medical school at University School of Medicine.

_____ Aaron pursued his dream by going to college.

Name_____   Date _____

Medical School, Version Two

Directions: Read "Medical School, Version Two" and answer the questions following the story in complete sentences.

When Aaron was in the eighth grade, he visited a doctor on Career Day and observed that being a doctor was a great way to help people. Aaron decided that he wanted to be a doctor some day. During high school Aaron took chemistry and biology classes. He also volunteered at a hospital. Then Aaron further pursued his dream by going to college.

At Mount Vernon College Aaron took a lot of chemistry and biology classes. Aaron worked very hard through college and earned good grades. After graduating from Mount Vernon College, Aaron began medical school at University School of Medicine. This is Aaron's third year in medical school. Now he is both working in a lab and taking classes.

Although he is in his third year of medical school, Aaron has not yet decided what type of doctor he would like to be. Aaron enjoys research and may decide to use his medical degree to do research or teach. Aaron is glad that he decided to attend medical school.

1. How is "Medical School, Version Two" different from "Medical School"?

   _____

   _____

   _____

2. Which version of the story do you like better? Why?

   _____

   _____

   _____

Mini-Lesson #5: Sequence

Teacher Lesson Plan

Objective

Students will practice sequencing the events of a story that uses flashbacks. Students will reflect on the meaning of *sequence* and *flashback*.

Summary

In this mini-lesson the teacher will begin with a review of sequence and flashbacks. Then the students will complete student activity sheets that require them to sequence events and to write about their understanding of sequence and flashback.

Materials

- "Mall Shopping" and "Sequence and Flashback" student activity sheets (1 copy per student, pages 18, 19)

Time: 20 minutes

Lesson

1. Introduction: Ask students to think back to the discussion and practice with sequence in Lesson 4. Ask students to explain what "sequence" and "flashback" are and how they relate to stories. (*Sequence is the chronological order of events that take place in a story. Flashbacks occur when a scene or event from the past is inserted into a story.*)

2. Ask students why flashbacks sometimes confuse readers about the sequence of events in a story. Assure students that with some concentration and practice, they will be able to enjoy and understand flashbacks in stories.

3. Ask students to share any examples of flashbacks that they have come across since the first Sequence Mini-Lesson.

4. Brainstorm with students a list of ideas about why authors may choose to use flashbacks. (*to make the story more interesting, to show that it's normal to occasionally flashback to a previous event when telling a story, to add variety to their writing, to give the background information that helps the reader understand a character's current situation, to add suspense to a story by keeping some details until later, etc.*)

5. Distribute "Mall Shopping" student activity sheets, review directions, and allow students to work independently. Review answers as time allows. *See the answer key below.*

More Practice

Create an "I Spotted a Flashback!" bulletin board. Provide note cards for students to write a brief description of flashbacks they notice during their independent reading times. Attach the note cards to the bulletin board for others to read.

Silent Reading Practice

Refer to page 82 for a corresponding reproducible student sheet and directions.

Answer Key (page 18)

3, 6, 2, 5, 4, 1—Bonus Question: Saturday

Name_____   **Date** _____

Mall Shopping

Directions: Read the following story and then number the events in the order in which they happened.

Hi! My name is Trista, AKA (also known as) Miss Mall Shopper! Every Saturday afternoon my best friend, Janessa, and I go to the local Graham Mall and shop. Today I found a really warm sweater to buy, but last week I bought some hiking boots. Shopping is always a great time with Janessa!

One day last year Janessa's mom took us to the Mega Mall to shop, and we had a blast! My mom gave me $50 to buy some jeans, and since I found some on clearance for $20 I was able to buy two pairs. Unfortunately, before I found the $20 clearance jeans, Janessa bought the exact same pair of jeans at a different store for $40. She was not happy! But it worked out okay because before we left the mall she returned the $40 jeans and got her money back. Then she was able to buy two pairs of the clearance jeans. I hope that we are able to go back to the Mega Mall this year!

_____ Trista bought two pairs of jeans for $20 each.

_____ Trista bought a new sweater.

_____ Janessa bought a pair of $40 jeans.

_____ Trista bought a pair of hiking boots.

_____ Janessa bought two pairs of $20 jeans.

_____ Janessa's mom took the girls shopping at the Mega Mall.

Bonus Question: Trista says, "Today I found a really warm sweater." What day of the week is "Today"?

_____

Name _____ **Date** _____

Sequence and Flashback

Directions: Answer the following questions in complete sentences.

1. What is *sequence*?

   _____

   _____

   _____

2. What is a *flashback*?

   _____

   _____

   _____

3. How do flashbacks affect the sequence of a story?

   _____

   _____

   _____

4. Why might an author use flashbacks?

   _____

   _____

   _____

Mini-Lesson #6: Setting

Teacher Lesson Plan

Objective

Students will create their own settings with words and pictures.

Summary

In this mini-lesson the teacher will lead students to understand that every story has a setting and that there are two basic parts to a setting. Students will complete a student activity sheet that asks them to create two different settings for a story.

Materials

- "Setting" student activity sheets (1 copy per student, page 21)
- chalkboard or chart paper and markers

Time: 20 minutes

Lesson

1. Introduction: Tell students that every story has a plot, characters, and setting. Explain to students that the plot is what happens in the story and the characters are the people or animals in the story. Ask students to share what they know about the setting of a story. Tell students that today they are going to create their own settings.

2. Tell students that the setting of a story has basically two parts: *where* and *when*. On the chalkboard or chart paper, draw a two-columned chart and write "where" above one column and "when" above the other. Explain to students that "where" can refer to a specific location (e.g., Jefferson City, Tennessee) or it can refer to a more general place (e.g., a house). Similarly, the "when" can refer to a specific time (the afternoon of January 5, 1954), or it can refer to a more general time period (past, present, or future).

3. Ask students to brainstorm possible settings on the chalkboard or chart paper with you. Remind students that their setting must include some type of "when" and "where." Encourage students to create a variety of settings.

4. Tell students that authors and illustrators provide a lot of details in a story through drawings and writing to let the reader know about the setting of the story. The more details a reader has, the easier it is to visualize the story in his or her head.

5. Distribute "Setting" student activity sheets and review directions. Give students time to complete their settings independently. If time allows, let students share their settings.

More Practice

Have students identify the setting of a book that you have read aloud in class. Discuss with students how the author helped them to know more about the setting. Have students create pictures or murals of how they envision the setting of the story. Discuss the similarities and differences between their interpretations.

Silent Reading Practice

Refer to page 83 for a corresponding reproducible student sheet and directions.

Setting

Directions: In the box below, draw a setting. You may use ideas from books that you have read, or you can create your own inventive new setting. Be creative and remember to give clues about "when" and "where" the setting is. Then on the lines below, write about your setting. Use descriptive words that will help the reader visualize the setting in his or her mind.

_____

_____

_____

_____

_____

_____

_____

Mini-Lesson #7: Setting

Teacher Lesson Plan

Objective

Students will write a description of a *setting*. Students will use the written description to draw a setting.

Summary

In this mini-lesson the teacher will review the two parts of the setting of a story (where and when). Then students will complete a student activity sheet that asks them to describe a setting in writing and then trade papers with a partner. The students will then draw a setting according to their partner's description.

Materials

- "Where and When?" student activity sheets (1 copy per student, page 23)

Time: 20 minutes

Lesson

1. Introduction: Ask students if they can remember the two basic parts of a setting. (*where and when the story takes place*)

2. Tell students that stories in books are not the only stories with settings. Movies, plays, and television shows all have settings too. Ask students to share the setting of a movie, play, or television show that they have seen recently.

3. Tell students that yesterday they both drew and wrote about their own setting ideas. Explain to students that today they will describe a setting in writing and then trade papers with a partner. The students will then each draw a setting according to each partner's written description.

4. Distribute "Where and When?" student activity sheets and give students time to write their descriptions. Then have the students trade papers with partners and draw a setting according to their partner's written description.

5. When students have completed their drawings, have them discuss with their partners how close their partner's drawings were to what they had in mind. Encourage them to discuss what was easy and what was difficult about drawing the setting. They should discuss whether their written descriptions gave enough details and which details would help a reader understand the setting the best.

6. Have students share their experiences and discussions with the class.

Literature Connections

Refer to page 90 for ideas on practice in recognizing the importance of setting with *When I Was Young in the Mountains* by Cynthia Rylant and *Peppe the Lamplighter* by Elisa Bartone.

Name_____

Date_____

Where and When?

Directions: Write a description of a setting on the lines below. Be sure to give details about both *where* and *when* the setting is. Then trade papers with a partner and see if your partner can draw the setting from your description.

_____

_____

_____

_____

_____

_____

_____

Mini-Lesson #8: Setting

Teacher Lesson Plan

Objective

Students will discuss how a setting affects the *mood* of a story. Students will create settings to incur specific moods.

Summary

In this mini-lesson the teacher will guide students to understand how the setting affects the mood of a story. The teacher will lead students in identifying the mood of example settings. Then the students will complete a student activity sheet that asks them to create settings that reflect a specific mood.

Materials

- overhead transparency or copies of "What's the Mood?" (page 25)
- "Setting and Story Mood" student activity sheets (1 copy per student, page 26)

Time: 20 minutes

Lesson

1. Introduction: Ask students what they think the "mood of a story" might mean. Explain that the mood of a story affects how a reader is supposed to feel when he or she reads a story. Authors often use the setting of the story to set the mood of the story.

2. Ask students how they think the author might make the setting of the story if the author wanted the story to have a scary mood (*a rainy dark night, in a dark forest or old creepy house*). Ask students what the setting may be like if the author wanted the story to have a happy mood (*a bright sunshiny afternoon in a beautiful garden or amusement park*).

3. Display an overhead transparency or distribute copies of "What's the Mood?" Explain to students that you will read the example settings together and then identify the mood of the story. (*Setting #1: scary or mysterious; Setting #2: hopeful or pleasant*)

4. Point out how the author of these settings used all of the senses but taste (sight, smell, sound, touch) to help describe the setting and set the mood.

5. Distribute "Setting and Story Mood" student activity sheets and review directions together. Allow students to work independently to complete the activity.

6. If time allows, invite students to read their settings and have the class guess what mood their setting was supposed to establish.

More Practice

Watch a brief movie or television show in class. Have students identify the setting and mood of the storyline. Discuss how the producers used the setting to set the mood of the story.

Name_____   **Date** _____

What's the Mood?

Directions: Read the following paragraphs which describe two different settings. Then write on the lines what type of mood the setting creates. Underline key words or phrases from the setting that made you think that.

Setting #1

The sun had been shining all day long until just a few minutes ago. Now the sky was completely dark except for an occasional streak of bright lightning. The air became chilly and damp. The rain poured down on the roof of the cabin, and the owls outside began to hoot.

What is the mood of Setting #1?

_____

_____

_____

Setting #2

This June had been especially beautiful. The trees were beginning to bud, and the birds were joyfully making their nests. The sky was a brilliant blue, and the clouds were as puffy as cotton balls. There was a smell of freshness in the air and the feeling of good things to come.

What is the mood of setting #2?

_____

_____

_____

Name_____   **Date** _____

Setting and Story Mood

Directions: Choose one of the following moods. Circle that mood and then create a setting that would develop that mood. Write a description of your setting on the lines below. Remember to include a "where" and a "when." Remember to use as many details as you can. Then draw a picture of your setting in the box below.

• scary • mysterious • excited • pleasant • sad • funny

_____

_____

_____

_____

_____

_____

_____

Mini-Lesson #9: Cause and Effect

Teacher Lesson Plan

Objective

Students will discuss the meaning of a *cause* and an *effect*. Students will complete a cause-and-effect chart.

Summary

In this mini-lesson the teacher will guide the students in a discussion of what "cause and effect" means. The class will practice creating some cause-and-effect situations together. Then students will independently complete a cause-and-effect chart that asks them to identify logical causes and effects.

Materials

- a single copy of "Cause-and-Effect Examples" (page 28) cut apart. ***Keep these for Cause-and-Effect Lesson #10***.
- "What Is the Cause? What Is the Effect?" student activity sheets (1 copy per student, page 29)
- chalkboard or chart paper and markers

Time: 20 minutes

Lesson

Prior to the lesson, photocopy and cut apart "Cause-and-Effect Examples."

1. Introduction: Tell students that you are going to begin looking at "Cause and Effect." Ask students what they know about "Cause and Effect." Help students to understand that a "cause" is an event that makes something else happen. An "effect" is an event that happens as a result, or effect, of something else that happened.

2. Tell students that you will practice matching causes and effects. Write "Cause" on the left side of the chalkboard or chart paper and write "Effect" on the right side. Show students the three cause-and-effect examples that you have copied and cut apart. Allow students to match the cause-and-effect statements and place them under the appropriate heading on the board or chart paper. (e.g., *Cause: My dog's leash broke. Effect: He ran away.*) Invite students to make up their own cause-and-effect examples.

3. Distribute "What Is the Cause? What Is the Effect?" student activity sheets and review directions together. Allow students to complete the activity independently. Invite students to share their ideas with a partner or a small group as time permits. Discuss the different causes and effects that students choose.

More Practice

Continue identifying cause-and-effect relationships as you study history. Discuss the causes and effects of a specific event in history. Have students create charts to show the cause-and-effect relationships of historical events.

Cause-and-Effect Examples

My dog's leash broke.
He ran away.
I forgot to put sugar in the lemonade.
It tasted very sour.
My sister gave me my favorite candy bar.
I was very happy.

Name_____   **Date** _____

What Is the Cause? What Is the Effect?

Directions: Complete the chart below. The left side of the chart is for causes, and the right side of the chart is for effects. Make sure that your answers make sense.

Cause	Effect
1. I tripped on the steps at school.	1. _____ _____ _____
2. _____ _____ _____	2. We were soaking wet!
3. I scored the winning goal in our soccer game.	3. _____ _____ _____
4. _____ _____ _____	4. My mom is very happy today.
5. I completed my homework.	5. _____ _____ _____

Mini-Lesson #10: Cause and Effect

Teacher Lesson Plan

Objective

Students will create their own cause-and-effect sentences.

Summary

In this mini-lesson the teacher will lead students in creating sentences that involve causes and effects. Students will create their own cause-and-effect sentences with the suggestions given on an activity sheet.

Materials

- "Cause-and-Effect Examples" and chart (from "Mini-Lesson #9: Cause and Effect")
- "Causes and Effects" student activity sheets (1 copy per student, pages 31, 32)
- chalkboard or chart paper and markers

Time: 20 minutes

Lesson

Prior to the lesson, secure the Cause-and-Effect Examples and chart that you created in the Cause and Effect: Mini-lesson #9. Make sure that the examples are paired and in the correct columns of the chart. (e.g., Cause: My dog's leash broke. Effect: He ran away.)

1. Introduction: Ask students to think back to the causes and effects they worked with in the previous lesson. Ask students what happens first—the cause or the effect. Display the "Cause-and-Effect Examples" chart (from the Cause and Effect Mini-Lesson #9).

2. Ask students to create sentences that include each cause with its appropriate effect. (e.g., My dog's leash broke, and then he ran away.) Have students write their sentences on the chalkboard or chart paper. Look at each sentence and ask students whether the cause or the effect is mentioned first in each sentence. Then ask students if they can now reverse the order of the cause and effect in the sentences. (*e.g., The dog ran away because his leash broke.*) Have students write these new sentences on the chalkboard or chart paper. Explain to students that sometimes the cause is mentioned first in the sentence and sometimes the effect is mentioned first. As good readers they must figure out which events are causes and which events are effects, regardless of where they are mentioned in a sentence.

3. Explain to students that they will now have the opportunity to create more of their own cause-and-effect sentences. Distribute "Causes and Effects" student activity sheets and review directions together. (*You may choose whether students' cause-and-effect sentences for this activity must be realistic or whether they may be silly. Let students know during the time you go over the directions.*) Allow students to work independently. You may choose to have students share their sentences aloud with the class or with a partner when the activity is completed.

More Practice

Continue practicing cause and effect by asking students to write autobiographies that identify different cause-and-effect events in their own lives.

Name _____ **Date** _____

Causes and Effects

Directions: Draw a line to match each cause to its effect. Then create two sentences for each of the first matched pairs. (One sentence should mention the cause first. One sentence should mention the effect first.)

Causes	Effects
• Ruth ate two bags of cotton candy.	• I gave him a round of applause.
• Kevin helped his dad make a cake.	• She got a very bad stomachache.
• Trudy practiced running every morning.	• His dad was proud.
• Zechariah sang a song with his dog.	• She won second place in the marathon race.

1. (Cause mentioned first)

_____

_____

(Effect mentioned first)

_____

_____

2. (Cause mentioned first)

_____

_____

(Effect mentioned first)

_____

_____

Name _____ **Date** _____

Causes and Effects *(cont.)*

Directions: Now create two sentences for each of the two remaining matched pairs on page 31. (One sentence should mention the cause first. One sentence should mention the effect first.)

3. (Cause mentioned first)

_____

_____

(Effect mentioned first)

_____

_____

4. (Cause mentioned first)

_____

_____

(Effect mentioned first)

_____

_____

Extra Credit: Compose four original sentences of cause and effect. After writing each one, rewrite it, reversing the order of cause and effect as you did for the previous four sentences.

_____

_____

_____

_____

_____

_____

Mini-Lesson #11: Cause and Effect

Teacher Lesson Plan

Objective

Students will read a short story and identify causes and effects within the story.

Summary

In this mini-lesson the teacher will guide students to see events in their own lives as cause-and-effect events. Students will complete a student activity sheet that requires them to read a short story about a boy's life and identify cause-and-effect events.

Materials

- chalkboard or chart paper and markers

- "Wayne the Victor, Part One" student activity sheets (1 copy per student, pages 34, 35)

Time: 20 minutes

Lesson

1. Introduction: Tell students that they experience many "cause and effect" events in their own lives. Ask students to share any examples they can think of in their own lives. You may want to share an example from your own life (*e.g., My wife was offered a better job in Ohio, so we moved to Ohio*). Create a new two-columned chart on the chalkboard or chart paper and label one column "Cause" and one column "Effect." Place each event under its appropriate category (*e.g., Cause: My wife was offered a better job in Ohio. Effect: We moved to Ohio*).

2. Assure students that being able to identify causes and effects will help make them better thinkers and better readers. Tell students that today they will read a short story about a boy's life. Assure students that if they read carefully they should be able to identify several causes and effects in the boy's life. Distribute "Wayne the Victor: Part One" student activity sheets and review directions together. Ask students what it means if the title says "Part One." (*There will be other parts; this is only the beginning part of the story.*) Depending upon students' current level of understanding, you may choose to complete this activity as a whole group, with partners, or independently. *See answer key below for suggested answers.*

More Practice

Use science experiments to practice recognizing cause-and-effect events. Identify the causes and effects of an experiment. Discuss how the effects would be different if the causes were changed.

Answer Key (page 35)

1. Wayne did not go to school.
2. He missed so much school.
3. He decided to start working on his attendance.
4. He did not think that his brother and mom cared about his decision.
5. He felt better.

Name _____   Date _____

Wayne the Victor: Part One

I used to miss school a lot. I'd be gone from school one or two days a week, and I really didn't have any excuses. Some days I was just tired or I didn't feel like going to school, so I didn't. Other times, I was mad at my teacher, or I felt like a failure and so I stayed home. When I was missing lots of school I didn't like school. It was hard to get to know people, and my teachers were frustrated with me. I was confused all the time and felt like I didn't belong. I felt like I'd never learn what people wanted me to learn.

Then I realized that I didn't like school because I was gone so much—I didn't give myself a chance to like school. I wasn't giving myself a chance to get to know people or figure out what was going on in my classes. I felt sad and mad inside. I realized I was giving up on myself and failing myself. I decided I was no longer going to give up on myself.

I chose to work on my school attendance first. I decided that no matter what, I was going to go to school every day. I told my brother about my new decision and he said he didn't care. I told my mom about my new decision and she said, "Okay, that's nice, Wayne," but I don't think she really cared either. I started feeling bad inside again because they didn't act proud or anything. So I told myself about my new decision, and then I told myself, "I am proud of you, Wayne! You can do it!" It may sound silly but it did make me feel better! I told myself that no matter how I felt or what my family or teachers thought, I had to make myself go to school everyday.

I wrote myself this reminder with big letters on a piece of notebook paper: **Go to School, Wayne! Don't give up on yourself! I am proud of you!** Then I taped it to the wall beside my bed so I'd see it every night and every morning. I made another sign just like it and taped it on the wall in the corner, close to the floor. I decided I would put my book bag in that corner every day when I came home from school and then it'd be easy to find each morning so I could take it to school with me. I had decided that I was going to quit giving up on myself and I was doing things to help myself be a victor.

Name_____   **Date** _____

Wayne the Victor: Part One *(cont.)*

Directions: Read "Wayne the Victor: Part One" carefully. Complete the chart below. The left side of the chart is for "causes." The right side of the chart is for "effects." Make sure that your answers make sense.

Cause	Effect
1. Some days Wayne was tired or just did not feel like going to school.	1. _____ _____ _____
2. _____ _____ _____	2. Wayne did not like school and it was hard to get to know people.
3. Wayne decided he was no longer going to give up on himself.	3. _____ _____ _____
4. _____ _____ _____	4. Wayne started feeling bad inside again.
5. Wayne told himself, "I am proud of you!"	5. _____ _____ _____.

Mini-Lesson #12: Cause and Effect

Teacher Lesson Plan

Objective

Students will identify the causes and effects of specific events of a short story.

Summary

In this mini-lesson the teacher will guide the students in a brief review of cause and effect, as well as a brief review of the story read in the previous lesson, "Wayne the Victor: Part One." Finally, the students will read "Wayne the Victor: Part Two" and complete a student activity sheet that asks them to fill in the blanks to identify causes and effects from the story.

Materials

- "Wayne the Victor: Part Two" student activity sheets (1 copy per student, pages 37, 38)

Time: 20 minutes

Lesson

1. Introduction: Ask a student to retell what happened in the story they read yesterday, "Wayne the Victor: Part One." Ask students to identify some of the cause-and-effect events in Wayne's life that they read about in "Wayne the Victor: Part One." Tell students that today they will read part two of the story and will note more cause-and-effect events in Wayne's life.

2. Distribute "Wayne the Victor: Part Two" student activity sheets and review directions. Allow students time to work independently. *See the suggested answers in the answer key below.*

More Practice

1. Practice identifying causes and effects by discussing the effects of different changes in the environment. Lead the class in a discussion of environmental issues and have students identify important causes and effects involved. Have students create murals that show the various causes and effects associated with a specific environmental problem.

2. Practice identifying causes and effects by inspecting mathematical story problems for cause-and-effect relationships. Point out to students that they can find cause-and-effect relationships in all different areas of their lives.

Silent Reading Practice

Refer to page 84 for corresponding reproducible student sheet and directions.

Answer Key (page 38)

1. He couldn't figure out how to do his schoolwork.
2. He started drawing on his desk.
3. The teacher made him stay in during recess as punishment for drawing on his desk.
4. He thought failure thoughts.
5. He fights failure thoughts with victory thoughts.

Name _____   **Date** _____

Wayne the Victor: Part Two

After I started making myself go to school every day, I realized I really didn't know what was going on in my class. I would hear the teacher explain what she wanted us to do, and I would watch the other kids do it, but I couldn't figure out how to do it. I started feeling like a failure again. I went home from school and threw my book bag in the corner and said, "I'm not going to school again!" Then I saw my signs, and I remembered that if I didn't go to school tomorrow, I'd be giving up on myself. I made myself go to school the next day.

In the middle of math class, I was so lost. So I started drawing on my desk. As soon as my teacher called my name, I remembered I wasn't supposed to draw on my desk. She made me stay in for recess. I was pretty mad about that, and inside my head I said to myself that *I'm not going to school tomorrow. I need a break from here, and I'm not learning anything anyway.* The sign from my bedroom wasn't there to remind me not to give up, so I kept thinking these failure thoughts the rest of the morning.

In the afternoon we had history class, and the teacher told us we were going to learn about the Civil War. I thought a war must be at least a little bit exciting, so I decided to listen. It turned out that the Civil War was very exciting, and the teacher said we'd get to do some role-play acting later in the week. I was thinking so much about history that I forgot about my failure thoughts for a while, and I actually started looking forward to coming to school tomorrow.

Now I look at my failure thoughts as my own war. When I feel like giving up on myself, there is a war going on inside of me. If I don't fight back, I'll lose the war. When failure thoughts attack my mind, I have to fight back with victory thoughts. For example, attack: *I'm not going to school tomorrow. This is dumb. I'll never understand this.* I fight back: *Don't give up on yourself, Wayne. You must go to school everyday. You have to keep trying, no matter how hard it gets.* I win the war. I become a victor.

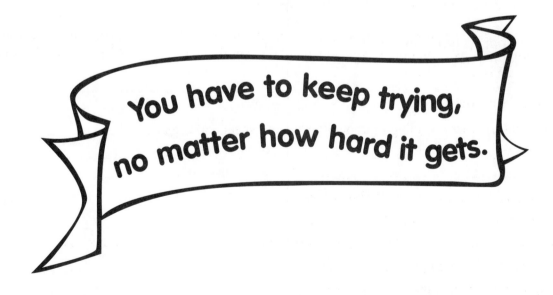

You have to keep trying, no matter how hard it gets.

Name_____ **Date** _____

Wayne the Victor: Part Two *(cont.)*

Directions: Read "Wayne the Victor: Part Two" and complete the chart below. The left side of the chart is for "causes." The right side of the chart is for "effects." Make sure that your answers make sense.

Cause	Effect
1. _____ _____ _____	1. He started feeling like a failure again.
2. In the middle of math class he was so lost.	2. _____ _____ _____
3. _____ _____ _____	3. He was pretty mad.
4. The sign from his bedroom wasn't there to remind him not to give up.	4. _____ _____ _____
5. _____ _____ _____	5. He became a victor.

Mini-Lesson #13: Cause and Effect

Teacher Lesson Plan

Objective

Students will read the final part of "Wayne the Victor" and then will answer questions concerning causes and effects in Wayne's life.

Summary

In this mini-lesson the teacher will guide the students in a brief review of the previous two parts of the "Wayne the Victor" story. Finally, students will read "Wayne the Victor: Part Three" and independently complete questions concerning causes and effects in Wayne's life.

Materials

- "Wayne the Victor: Part Three" student activity sheets (1 copy per student, pages 40, 41)

Time: 20 minutes

Lesson

1. Introduction: Ask students to think of a sentence that involves a cause-and-effect relationship. (For example, I was late for school because I could not find my shoes.) Discuss which event in the sentence is the cause and which event is the effect. Assure students that they have many causes and effects in their lives, just like Wayne in the story that they have been reading.

2. Tell students that today they will read the final part of "Wayne the Victor." Ask students to recall some of the previous cause-and-effect events in Wayne's life. Invite students to make predictions about what they think may happen in the last part of "Wayne the Victor."

3. Explain that instead of a chart, today students will be asked to answer questions that ask for the causes or effects of events mentioned in the story. Distribute "Wayne the Victor: Part Three" student activity sheets and review directions. *See answer key below.*

More Practice

Create a bulletin board to reinforce "Cause and Effect." Title the bulletin board "Causes and Effects in Our Lives." Have students draw or write about one feeling that they have (*happy, sad, proud, excited, surprised*). Then have students draw or write about what causes them to feel this way. Display students' work and discuss the different cause-and-effect relationships represented.

Answer Key (page 41)

1. He chooses to do what's right, even when it's not easy.
2. He put a sign in his notebook.
3. When he's working hard at something and still can't understand it.
4. He thinks he's giving up on himself if he doesn't at least try it.
5. He's proud of himself and gives himself a "V."

Wayne the Victor: Part Three

Now you're probably wondering what makes me a victor. Is it because I get good grades in school? No, not really. My grades aren't all that good. Is it because everyone at school likes me? No, I'm still not friends with too many people. Then why am I a victor? I'm a victor because I choose to do what's right even when it's not easy. I choose to go to school every day because it's right, even if I really don't want to go. I made myself that promise. I choose to think victor thoughts instead of failure thoughts. I decided to do that. And my latest decision was that I wasn't going to cheat—no matter what.

Sign #2: **Wayne, don't cheat, no matter what! Don't give up on yourself!** I put that sign in my notebook after our teacher gave us a lecture about not cheating. Although I don't like to admit it, what she said really made sense! If I cheat, I'm giving up on myself again! I'm saying to myself, *Wayne's not good enough so I have to steal someone else's ideas*. I am good enough! I don't need to steal someone else's work. I decided I'd rather get D's and know that it was my own work than get A's and know that it was someone else's work.

The wars started up in my head again but I am determined to win. When I am tempted to cheat, I fight back with my victory thoughts and make myself keep working. Sometimes when I'm working really hard at something and still not getting it, I go ask my teacher for help. She explains it to me again and I think about it some more, and then lots of times I can finish my work easily. I never go ask the teacher for help without trying the work several times on my own though. To me, that's giving up— failing myself. I have to give myself a chance.

Sometimes I still get F's, but sometimes I get B's and C's. When I work really hard on something, I'm proud of myself even if I don't get an "A." I've started sort of grading my own work. If something's really hard and I just want to cheat or quit, but I fight those thoughts and keep working hard at it, I give myself the grade "V." V is for *Victor*.

Don't Cheat—No Matter What !

Name_____

Date _____

Wayne the Victor: Part Three *(cont.)*

Directions: Read "Wayne the Victor: Part Three" and answer the following questions in complete sentences.

1. What causes Wayne to be a "Victor"?

   _____

   _____

   _____

2. What did Wayne do as a result of his teacher's lecture on not cheating?

   _____

   _____

   _____

3. What causes Wayne to go ask his teacher for help?

   _____

   _____

   _____

4. Why does Wayne never go ask the teacher for help without trying the work several times on his

   own?_____

   _____

   _____

5. When Wayne works really hard on something, what is the effect?

   _____

   _____

   _____

Mini-Lesson #14: Cause and Effect

Teacher Lesson Plan

Objective

Students will read a short story and answer questions that lead the students to identify specific causes and effects of several events in the story.

Summary

In this mini-lesson the teacher will guide the students in a brief review of cause and effect. Then students will complete a student activity sheet that asks them to read a short story and answer questions dealing with causes and effects of the story.

Materials

- "The Crash" student activity sheets (1 copy per student, pages 43, 44)

Time: 20 minutes

Lesson

1. Introduction: Tell students that before they begin their activity today you would like to review some things they have learned about causes and effects. Lead students in a discussion of the following questions:

   - What is a cause? What is an effect?
   - What comes first—a cause or an effect? Explain what you mean.
   - Do we only find cause-and-effect events on reading work sheets? Where else can we find cause-and-effect events?

2. Remind students that there are many cause-and-effect events in their lives everyday. It is important for them to always be thinking of the causes and effects of their own actions and the actions of others. Tell students that today they will read about some causes and effects of Jessica's afternoon.

3. Distribute "The Crash" student activity sheets and review directions. Make sure that students understand how to underline the information requested in numbers 1–4. Allow students time to work independently. *Note the suggested answers in the answer key below.*

More Practice

Have students read newspaper articles and look for cause-and-effect events mentioned throughout the articles.

Answer Key (page 44)

1. He was in an especially happy mood.
2. Her favorite song came on the radio.
3. A dog ran out in the middle of the street and she did not want to hit it.
4. She crashed into her neighbors' trash cans.

5. Answers will vary.
6. Answers will vary.

Name _____   **Date** _____

The Crash

Directions: Read "The Crash" carefully. Follow the directions for each question on page 44 and answer the questions in complete sentences.

The Crash

It was a bright and sunny day when Jessica got into the car. She rolled down the window and turned up the radio. Jessica could not believe that her father was finally letting her drive his car. Jessica had gotten her driver's license a month ago, but her dad was very protective of his car and refused to let her drive it anywhere. Today, however, her father was in an especially happy mood and agreed that she could use his car for the afternoon. Now Jessica was happily headed for her best friend Jacquie's house.

As Jessica pulled out of the driveway, her favorite song came on, and so she turned up the volume of the radio. Just as she pulled onto the road, a dog ran out in the middle of the street. Jessica swerved to miss the dog and ended up running into the neighbors' trash cans. Oh, no! Jessica thought. *Now Dad will never let me drive his car!*

Name_____   **Date** _____

The Crash *(cont.)*

Directions: Read "The Crash" carefully. Follow the directions for each question and answer the questions in complete sentences.

1. Underline the sentence in "The Crash" that says Jessica's father agreed to let her use his car for the afternoon. Answer the question below:

   What caused Jessica's father to let her drive his car for the afternoon?

   _____

   _____

   _____

2. Underline the sentence in "The Crash" that says Jessica turned up the volume to her radio. Answer the question below:

   What caused Jessica to turn up the volume of her radio? _____

   _____

   _____

3. Underline the sentence in "The Crash" that says Jessica swerved the car and then answer the question below:

   What caused Jessica to swerve? _____

   _____

   _____

4. Underline the part of the story where Jessica thinks that her father will never let her drive his car again. Answer the question below:

   What caused Jessica to think that her father would never let her drive his car again?

   _____

   _____

   _____

5. What caused Jessica to crash?_____

   _____

   _____

6. What are some of the possible effects of Jessica crashing into the neighbors' trash cans?

   _____

   _____

   _____

Mini-Lesson #15: Cause and Effect

Teacher Lesson Plan

Objective

Students will read a short story and then complete a chart that shows how cause-and-effect events can happen in a series.

Summary

In this mini-lesson the teacher will use dominos to show students how cause-and-effect events often happen as a chain of events. Then students will read a short story and complete a chart to show how events cause and affect each other.

Materials

- dominoes
- "The Runner" student activity sheets (1 copy per student, pages 46, 47))
- chalkboard or chart paper and marker

Time: 20 minutes

Lesson

1. Introduction: Set up the dominoes in a row so that when the first domino is tapped, it will begin the chain reaction to knock down all dominoes. Tap the first domino and then ask students how the dominoes are like cause-and-effect events. (*The first domino caused the second domino to fall, which caused the third domino to fall, and so forth. The first domino is a cause; the last domino is an effect. All of the others could be considered both a cause and an effect of the chain reaction. Similarly, events often happen in a chain reaction pattern. Some events cause other events, which cause other events, and so on. Sometimes an event can be both a cause and an effect.*)

2. Tell students that in the previous activities they focused on cause-and-effect pairs. Today they will focus on how some events happen in a chain reaction pattern, which are both causes and effects. Show students an example on the chalkboard or chart paper. First write the first event: "It rained for two hours." Then ask students what might happen as an effect of it having rained for two hours. Write this event underneath the first event. (*e.g., The river flooded.*) Ask students what might happen as an effect of that and write it below the second event. (*e.g., Many people's basements flooded.*) Show students how sometimes events can be both cause and effect events. They happen in a chain of events, similar to our dominoes.

3. Distribute "The Runner" student activity sheets and review directions. Complete the activity together as a whole group or allow students to work independently. Students' answers may vary.

More Practice

Have students work in groups to complete flow charts that show the causes and effects of these events: *The temperature fell to three degrees below zero; Ricky won first place in the art contest; Shirley received a letter from the president of the United States.*

Name _____ **Date** _____

Directions: Read "The Runner" carefully and then complete the chart on page 47.

The Runner

When Bradley saw his cousin compete in the State Racing Championships, he began to dream that he would one day compete in the State Racing Championships. Since his dream was so strong, Bradley began to organize races in his neighborhood on the weekends with other neighborhood kids. To prepare for these neighborhood races, Bradley would run every day after school. Sometimes he even borrowed his grandma's stopwatch and timed himself.

When Bradley began middle school, he signed up to be on the track team. Bradley had to run and practice very hard to stay on the track team, but he wanted to compete in the State Racing Championship so much that he kept working hard. Three years later Bradley successfully tried out for the high school track team. Bradley realized that he not only had to work hard at running, but he also had to work hard at his schoolwork. All members of the track team had to keep their grades up so that they could continue to play.

Bradley kept his grades up and proved that he was a committed student and track team member. When he was a senior in high school he had the opportunity to compete in the Regional Racing Championships . . . and he won! One month later he was fulfilling his dream by competing in the State Racing Championships.

On the day of the State Racing Championships, Bradley was very nervous. He knew he would be competing against some of the best runners in the state, but he decided that he needed to focus on his own running and not worry about the other runners. All of Bradley's years of hard work finally paid off when he brought home the State Racing Championships second-place trophy.

Name_____   Date _____

The Runner *(cont.)*

Directions: Carefully read "The Runner" and complete the chart below. Write one cause-and-effect event in each box in the order they occurred. You will not need to use every cause-and-effect event.

Cause	
Effect	

Cause	
Effect	

Cause	
Effect	

Cause	
Effect	

Cause	
Effect	

Mini-Lesson #16: Prediction

Teacher Lesson Plan

Objective

Students will define *prediction* and practice making logical predictions.

Summary

In this mini-lesson the teacher will guide the students in creating a definition for *predict*. Then students will read a letter about Belize and use a prediction chart to record their predictions about what information will be included in the next letter, as well as an explanation of what helped them to make their predictions.

Materials

- chart paper (2 pieces)
- "Belize?" student activity sheets (1 copy per student, pages 49, 50)

Time: 20 minutes

Lesson

1. Introduction: Ask students what it means to *predict*. Write a definition on chart paper. (You may guide students to a definition similar to this: *Predict—to use observations or experiences to make a reasonable guess about what will happen.*) Tell students that good readers predict a lot while they read a story. Tell students that we are going to practice predicting today with a short story.

2. Write the title of today's reading selection on the board (*Belize?*). Ask students what they can predict about the reading selection from the title. Why do they think the title has a question mark after it? Tell students that they have very little information about the reading selection but many times you can make fair predictions just by the title of a story. Ask students what would make it easier for them to make predictions (*a picture with the title, a brief introduction, etc.*). Ask students if they know what Belize (b-'lEz) is. Assure students that Belize is a country and that they will have to read the selection to find out any more information.

3. Distribute "Belize?" student activity sheet and review directions together. Explain that the information for the right side of the chart, "Reasons Why I Made the Prediction" should include information from Julia's first letter, "Belize?" Distribute activity sheets and allow students time to work. *See possible answers below.*

Possible Answers (page 50)	
I predict Julia will write about what "plantain" is.	Julia says, "Have you ever heard of plantain? Then she says she guesses we don't, and she wants to tell us more about Belize.
I predict Julia will write about the schools.	Julia says she has visited schools in Belize, and she probably thinks we are interested in them.

Name_____   **Date**_____

Belize?

September 22, 2003

Dear Friend,

Greetings! My name is Julia, and I am fifteen years old. Two years ago I went to Belize to visit friends with my parents. I had a blast and learned a lot! Do you know where Belize is? Have you ever heard of plantain? Do you know what a tapir is? Have you ever tasted corn ice cream? I am guessing that your answer was "no" to most of those questions, and that is why I am writing this letter to you. Belize has a lot of great things that not too many kids know about. I hope that my letters will help you learn more about this great country!

First of all, I should tell you where in the world Belize is. Belize is a country in Central America. Mexico and Guatemala are Belize's neighbors. I will try and tell you more about them later. The capital city of Belize is Belmopan, located in the center of the country. We spent most of our time in the large city of Belize City and the small town of San Ignacio.

Belize has many beautiful sights, but one of my favorite things about Belize is the people! I was able to visit several schools and churches in Belize and hang out with our old and new friends. So what do kids do for fun in Belize? Some kids probably do a lot of the same things that you do. Our friends' kids go to school on the weekdays, go to church on the weekend, help their parents with work at home, play ball with their friends, and buy sweets at the store.

There are many more things that I want to tell you about Belize and my experiences, but that will have to be kept for the next letter.

So long,

Julia

Name_____ **Date** _____

Belize? *(cont.)*

Directions: Carefully read "Belize?" and then complete the prediction chart below with your predictions about what Julia's next letter will contain. Write your predictions on the left side of the chart. On the right side of the chart, write what caused you to think of the predictions.

Predictions About What Julia Will Write in Her Second Letter	Reasons Why I Made the Predictions
1.	1.
2.	2.
3.	3.
4.	4.
5.	5.

Mini-Lesson #17: Prediction

Teacher Lesson Plan

Objective

Students will recall the definition of *predict*, and will continue making logical predictions.

Summary

In this mini-lesson the teacher will review the class definition of *predict*, and students will read the second letter from Julia about Belize. Students will evaluate their previous predictions and make new ones.

Materials

- "Belize #2" student activity sheets (1 copy per student, pages 52, 53)

Time: 20 minutes

Lesson

1. Introduction: Ask students if they remember our definition of *predict*. Discuss why it is important for readers to make predictions as they read. (*Making predictions helps readers focus on what they are reading and helps them to become more involved with what they are reading. Making predictions also helps readers understand the meaning of the text and notice details along the way.*)

2. Ask a student to tell about the letter "Belize?" that they read in the previous lesson. Invite students to share some of the predictions that they made concerning the second letter.

3. Tell students that today they will read the second letter from Julia about Belize. They will need to check to see if any of their predictions were correct, and then they will need to make new predictions. Tell students that you will have a brief discussion time after they finish their activity sheets today.

4. Distribute student activity sheets, review directions, and allow students time to work independently.

5. When students have completed the activity, ask them to share some predictions that they had made about the second letter that turned out to be correct. Then have students share some predictions that they had made about the second letter that turned out to be incorrect. Ask students to share what made it easy to predict some things and not so easy to predict other things. Tell students that they will have one more letter from Julia about Belize.

Literature Connections

Refer to page 90 for ideas on practicing predictions with *Peppe the Lamplighter* by Elisa Bartone and *Two Bad Ants* By Chris Van Allsburg.

Silent Reading Practice

Refer to page 85 for corresponding reproducible student sheet and directions.

Belize #2

September 27, 2003

Dear Friend,

While we were in Belize, we went to the Belize City Zoo—and it was awesome! It almost felt like you were right in the wildlife with all the animals. My favorite animal that we saw was the tapir. The tapir is the national animal of Belize. A tapir is a hoofed mammal, and it looks a little bit like a mix between a rhinoceros and a hog. It's sort of hard to describe   so you'll just have to look it up and find a picture for yourself.

When we got back to San Ignacio, my dad gave me money to buy an ice cream at the ice cream stand. They had all different kinds of flavors   chocolate chip, coconut, strawberry, and many more. The flavor that sounded interesting to me, though, was corn, so I decided to try it. Guess what it was? Yep, ice cream with corn in it   and I liked it!

We spent the rest of the day in San Ignacio. San Ignacio is a nice town. Most of the streets are dirt, and most of the houses are made of concrete blocks. A lot of the houses do not have hot water faucets, so you have to get used to cold showers. It was really tough at first, but sometimes after a hot day it feels okay. We walked most of the places we went, but when it's too far to walk we took the bus or got a ride from our friend who has a car. It's kind of nice to just enjoy the outdoors and some good company as you walk downtown or to the corner store.

There's one last thing that I want to tell you about in this letter: plantain. Plantain is a lot like bananas. There are quite a few plantain trees in San Ignacio. Our friends like to fix long, thin slices of fried plantain . We like it too!

Well, it appears that I am almost out of paper, so I will close. I hope that you are getting very interested in Belize! Remember to go look up a picture of a tapir!

Sincerely,

Julia

Name_____   **Date** _____

Belize #2 *(cont.)*

Directions: Carefully read "Belize #2" and then complete the prediction chart below with your predictions about what Julia's next letter will contain. Write your predictions on the left side of the chart. On the right side of the chart, write what caused you to think of those predictions.

Predictions About What Julia Will Write in Her Third Letter	Reasons Why I Made the Predictions
1.	1.
2.	2.
3.	3.
4.	4.
5.	5.

Mini-Lesson #18: Prediction

Teacher Lesson Plan

Objective

Students will reflect upon their predictions made during the Belize letters.

Summary

In this mini-lesson the teacher will lead students in a discussion of how authors help readers to make predictions. Students will then read the final letter from Julia about Belize and complete a student activity sheet that asks them to reflect on their predictions and what they have learned about prediction.

Materials

- "Belize #3" student activity sheets (1 copy per student, pages 55, 56)

Time: 20 minutes

Lesson

1. Introduction: Ask a student to remind the class of why good readers make predictions as they read. Ask students why it is important for readers to make predictions. Ask students how authors help readers to make predictions. (*The author gives the reader clues or uses situations with which readers are familiar. The author helps you to understand characters so that you will be able to predict what they might do next.*)

2. Ask a student to share what Julia wrote about in her second letter. Ask students to share what predictions they made for the third letter.

3. Distribute "Belize #3" and review directions with students. Allow students time to work independently.

More Practice

Make a prediction chart to use during read-aloud time. Add students' predictions to the chart as you read through the book. You may also want to label the students' predictions with their initials to encourage each one to contribute to the chart. Refer back to the chart to note predictions that were correct and those that were incorrect. Encourage students to understand that even if their predictions were incorrect, it was good for them to be active readers making predictions.

Belize #3

September 28, 2003

Dear Friend,

I regret to inform you that this will be the last letter that I will be able to write to you about Belize. There is still so much more left to tell you! I guess you will just have to do some research on your own to answer some of your remaining questions.

I decided that I must tell you something about some of the schools in Belize. The school that our friends' children attend is a private school. They have classes there from Infant 1 through Standard 4. This would be similar to U.S. schools that have kindergarten through 5th grade classes. The students and teachers wear uniforms at the school, but this is true of all of the schools in Belize. Some schools have as long as one hour and a half for lunch break, and many of the students go home to eat lunch. At recess many of the girls played jacks, and they were very good at it!

Belize has a lot of great sites and new things to experience, and it was sad to leave when our trip was over. Of course, what I will miss the most is my new friends and my old friends in Belize. Fortunately, though, we can keep in contact through letters and e-mail. I also predict that since I love Belize and my friends so much, I will be back to visit again many times in my life.

I hope that you have learned something new about Belize from my letters, and I hope you will be inspired to do some of your own research to learn even more about Belize. Who knows, perhaps one day you will go visit Belize as well!

So long,

Julia

Name_____   **Date** _____

Belize #3 *(cont.)*

Directions: Carefully read "Belize #3" and then answer the following questions in complete sentences.

1. What is one prediction you can make about what you think Julia would write next if she were to write another letter? What makes you think that?

   _____

   _____

   _____

2. Why is it important for readers to make predictions while they read?

   _____

   _____

   _____

3. What is one thing that you wish Julia had told you more about? How could you find information about that?

   _____

   _____

   _____

Mini-Lesson #19: Inference

Teacher Lesson Plan

Objective

Students will define *infer* and practice making inferences with a student activity sheet.

Summary

In this mini-lesson the teacher will guide students to create a definition for *infer*. Then students will listen to the story "Lena" and then make an inference. Finally, students will complete a student activity sheet that will help them to practice making inferences.

Materials

- chart paper and markers
- overhead transparency or copies of "Lena" story (page 58)
- "Changes" student work sheet (1 copy per student, page 59)

Time: 20 minutes

Lesson

1. Introduction: Ask students if they are familiar with the word *infer*. Write a definition for *infer* on the chart paper. (*Infer: to make a conclusion after considering all the facts.*) Explain to students that inferring is almost like being a detective. Tell students that good readers make inferences while they read. Explain that predictions and inferences are very similar because when you predict and infer, you are using clues to figure things out. Tell students that we will practice making inferences today.

2. Tell students that you will read aloud to them a story called "Lena." Explain to students that the story does not directly say what Lena's job is, but the story does give readers enough clues to infer what Lena does. Tell students that you will read the passage to them and then they will identify the facts from the story about what Lena does. Finally, they will come to a conclusion—an inference about what Lena's job is. Display the overhead or distribute copies of "Lena." *See Inference About Lena below for suggested answers.*

3. Explain to students that they will now practice making inferences on their own. Distribute the "Changes" student activity sheets and review directions together.

Inference About Lena

Facts from the story: She entered her office. She put down her briefcase. She had phone messages from people. She took notes as she talked to people on the phone. She called people and asked them questions. She typed up her notes from talking to the people. She said, "Now that's news!" She said, "This'll be great for the front page!"

Conclusion/Inference: Lena is a journalist for the newspaper.

Silent Reading Practice

Refer to page 86 for corresponding reproducible student sheet and directions.

Name_____   **Date** _____

Lena

Directions: Read "Lena" and then record facts from the story that give you clues as to what Lena's job is. Finally, make an inference about what Lena's job is.

> When Lena entered her office, she put down her briefcase and anxiously listened to her answering machine messages. She jotted down the phone numbers of the three people who called, grabbed her notebook and pen, and dialed the first number on her list. "Wow! Really? They found it in the backyard? Now, that's news!" she said. Lena asked the caller a series of questions and feverishly took notes as the person answered the questions. After making all of her calls, Lena began typing up the information she had gained. "This'll be great for the front page!" she exclaimed.

Clues (*facts from the story*)

_____

_____

_____

_____

_____

_____

Inference (*conclusion about what Lena's job is*)

_____

_____

_____

_____

_____

_____

Name_____   **Date** _____

Changes

Directions: The following story gives you many clues about what Daryl and his family are planning to do. Read the story carefully and then answer the questions that follow it.

Daryl couldn't believe the day was finally here! His mother woke him up early and rushed him to breakfast. "Make sure you wash your own bowl and put it back, Daryl," his mother said, "I don't want dirty dishes left behind." Daryl reached into a box filled with newspaper-wrapped dishes and pulled out a bowl for his breakfast.

As Daryl finished washing his dish, his best friend, Larry, came to the back door. "Hey, Daryl! I thought I'd better bring this sweatshirt over to you", he explained. "You left it at my house awhile back. It might be awhile before I see you again."

"Thanks," Daryl replied with a smile. "I wondered what happened to that."

"Yeah, and you're probably going to really need it now," Larry stated. "No more beach clothes for you!"

"Yeah," said Daryl, "But I'm ready for a change."

---

1. What can you infer from this story? What are Daryl and his family getting ready to do? (Be as specific as you can.)

_____

_____

_____

2. What clues helped you to make this inference? List at least three specific clues from the story.

_____

_____

_____

Mini-Lesson #20: Inference

Teacher Lesson Plan

Objective

Students will practice making *observations* and *inferences* and differentiating between them.

Summary

In this mini-lesson the teacher will review the concept of inference, and then students will complete an activity that asks them to make observations and inferences about a picture.

Materials

- "What's She Up To?" student activity sheets (1 copy per student, pages 61, 62)
- chalkboard or chart paper and markers

Time: 20 minutes

Lesson

1. Introduction: Ask a student to remind the class of the definition of *inference*. Remind students that using observations and clues is an important part of making inferences. Tell students that yesterday they practiced inferring with a story. Today they will practice inferring with a picture. Tell students that observations are things that are clearly stated or pictured in a book—the facts. Inferences are conclusions made after considering all the facts.

2. Distribute "What's She Up To?" student activity sheets and review directions together. Allow the students time to record their observations and inferences independently. *See Example Answers below.*

3. When students are finished, invite them to share their observations and inferences with the class. You may want to keep a list of their observations and inferences on the chalkboard or chart paper.

More Practice

Point out to students how we often use another person's body language to infer how he or she is feeling. You can usually tell what kind of a mood someone is in just by the way that person acts—you do not have to wait to be told what kind of a mood that person is in. Have students work in groups to create a skit that gives enough clues for the audience to infer what is going on or how the characters feel. Remind students that they want the audience to be able to make an inference, and an inference is a conclusion that is made after considering all the facts—inferences are not directly stated.

Literature Connection

Refer to page 90 for more inference practice with *"The Window"* by Jeannie Baker and *"Yo! Yes?"* by Chris Raschka.

Example Answers

Inference #1: I infer that the young lady is going to school.

Evidence: She has a book bag on the bench beside her. The girl is dressed in khakis and a button-up shirt.

Name_____

Date _____

What's She Up To?

Directions: Study the picture below. Record your observations and then make inferences about what is happening in the picture.

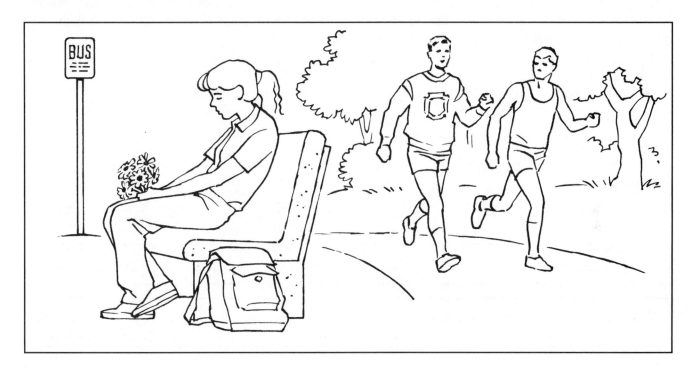

My Observation

_____

_____

_____

_____

_____

_____

_____

_____

Name _____   **Date:** _____

What's She Up To? *(cont.)*

My Inferences

What can you infer about the young lady on the bench? Where do you infer that she has been? Where do you infer that she is going? Use the observations that you recorded as evidence to support your inferences. Use complete sentences for your responses.

Inference #1

_____

_____

Evidence

_____

_____

_____

Inference #2

_____

_____

Evidence

_____

_____

_____

Inference #3

_____

_____

Evidence

_____

_____

_____

Mini-Lesson #21: Fact and Opinion

Teacher Lesson Plan

Objective

Students will differentiate between a *fact* and an *opinion*.

Summary

In this mini-lesson the teacher will guide the students in defining *fact* and *opinion*. Then the teacher will guide the students in creating some fact-and-opinion statements, after which the students will complete a student activity sheet that asks them to write their own fact-and-opinion statements.

Materials

- "Facts and Opinions" student activity sheets (1 copy per student, pages 64, 65)
- chalkboard or chart paper and markers

Time: 20 minutes

Lesson

1. Introduction: Ask students the difference between a fact and an opinion. Guide students to understand that a fact is something that you can prove, and an opinion is someone's idea, but one may not be able to prove it. With students, create a list of facts and opinions on the chalkboard or chart paper.

2. Tell students that facts are things that you can look up in a book or things that you can see. Many times facts include specific details or numbers. (*Show how your example facts on the chalkboard or chart paper use specific details or numbers.*) Tell students that many times opinions are just people's ideas, feelings, or preferences. (*Show how your example opinions on the chalkboard or chart paper show people's ideas, feelings, or preferences.*)

3. Show the students an object in the room. (*book, clock, desk, etc.*) Together, make a list of facts and opinions about this object.

4. Tell students that for their activity sheets they will be creating their own facts and opinions. Distribute student activity sheets and review directions together. Complete one fact and opinion together as an example. Allow students to work independently.

More Practice

Have a "Fact-and-Opinion Show and Tell." Give each student a brown paper lunch bag and a note card. For homework, have each student choose an object at home (one which they are permitted to bring to school in their brown paper lunch bag). Have students write two facts and two opinions about their object on the note card and then bring the object and note card back to school in the brown paper bag. Have students show-and-tell about their objects, using the facts and opinions on their note cards. Or display the items at the front of the classroom and read the fact-and-opinion note cards aloud to the class as they guess which item it matches.

Fact and Opinion

Name _____   **Date** _____

Facts and Opinions

Directions: Look at the scene below and on page 65. Write two facts and two opinions about each picture on the lines provided.

Scene #1

Fact for Scene #1:

_____

_____

Fact for Scene #1:

_____

_____

Opinion for Scene #1:

_____

_____

Opinion for Scene #1:

_____

_____

Name _____   **Date** _____

Facts and Opinions *(cont.)*

Scene #2

Fact for Scene #2:

_____

_____

Fact for Scene #2:

_____

_____

Opinion for Scene #2:

_____

_____

Opinion for Scene #2:

_____

_____

Mini-Lesson #22: Fact and Opinion

Teacher Lesson Plan

Objective

Students will differentiate between a *fact* and an *opinion*.

Summary

In this mini-lesson the teacher will guide the students in a discussion of whether *true* and *false* are the same as *fact* and *opinion*. The students will complete a student activity sheet that asks them to identify facts and opinions and to explain their reasoning behind their choices.

Materials

- "Some Facts and Some Opinions" student activity sheet (1 copy per student, page 67)

Time: 20 minutes

Lesson

1. Introduction: Lead students in a discussion of fact and opinion with the following questions:

   - Are *fact* and *opinion* the same as *true* and *false*?
   - Are all facts *true*, or can a fact be *false*?

   Guide students to understand that fact and opinion are not the same as true and false. Some so-called facts can be proven false. Just because a statement is recorded as a fact, it is not necessarily true. "Facts" can be proven true or false. Opinions can be *argued*, but they cannot be proven true or false.

2. Share with students some examples of "facts" that might be false. (*e.g., I am eight feet tall. The temperature today is 70° below zero.*) Discuss how these statements are facts because they can be proven. Discuss how these facts could be proven false.

3. Distribute "Some Facts and Some Opinions" student activity sheets. Review directions with students and allow students to work independently.

4. If time allows, review answers and have students defend their choices.

More Practice

Encourage students to write down facts and opinions that they find during their silent reading time. Or send students on a scavenger hunt to see how many facts and opinions they can find throughout the classroom in a given amount of time.

Silent Reading Practice

Refer to page 87 for corresponding reproducible student sheet and directions.

Answer Key (page 67)						
1. opinion	2. fact	3. opinion	4. fact	5. fact	6. fact	7. fact

Fact and Opinion

Name _____   **Date** _____

Some Facts and Some Opinions

Directions: Read the statements below. On the line beside each statement, write "Fact" if it can be proven (remember that "facts" can be proven true or false). Write "Opinion" if the statement is just someone's idea and cannot be proven.

_____ 1. Ohio is the best state in the United States.

_____ 2. More people live in Chicago than in the entire state of Texas.

_____ 3. Today is a beautiful day.

_____ 4. In the fall the grass turns blue.

_____ 5. I was born on December 8, 1989.

_____ 6. Sasha can run the 50-yard dash faster than any other kid in our school.

_____ 7. Last year October was the coldest month of the year.

Directions: Answer the following questions in complete sentences.

8. Choose one of the "fact" statements above and explain how you know that it is a fact.

_____

_____

_____

_____

9. Choose one of the "opinion" statements above and explain how you know that it is an opinion.

_____

_____

_____

_____

Mini-Lesson #23: Fact and Opinion

Teacher Lesson Plan

Objective

Students will play a game that requires them to identify statements as facts or opinions.

Summary

In this mini-lesson the teacher will lead the students in a game of bingo that requires them to decide if statements are facts or opinions.

Materials

- "Fact-and-Opinion Bingo" playing card (1 per student) (There are six different "Fact-and-Opinion Bingo" playing cards on pages 69–71. Each student should have only one playing card.)
- Bingo chips, beans, or paper clips to use for bingo game (You could also have students use pencils for the game and play it only once.)
- Fact-and-Opinion Bingo Statements (below)

Time: 20 minutes

Lesson

1. Introduction: Ask a student to remind the class how to tell whether a statement is a "fact" or an "opinion." Ask students if "fact and opinion" are the same as "true and false."

2. Explain to the students that today they will be playing Fact-and-Opinion Bingo. Tell students that they will each get a Fact-and-Opinion Bingo playing card. Explain that the cards all have the same items on them but that they are arranged in different ways on different cards. Tell students that you will read a statement that is either a fact or an opinion about a topic. Students should find the square on their card that correctly matches the statement and cover it. When students have covered four squares in a horizontal or vertical row, they should call out "Fact-and-Opinion Bingo!"

3. Distribute materials and begin the game. Repeat the game if desired.

Fact-and-Opinion Bingo Statements

- The Rocky Mountains go through Colorado.
- Soccer is the best sport in the world.
- There are more fast food restaurants in Kentucky than in any other state.
- A cat is the best animal to have for a pet.
- More high school students read fiction books than nonfiction books.
- Fall is the worst season of them all.
- Massachusetts is the best state to go for a vacation.
- On Thursdays more people in our school eat pizza than any other food.
- Rain is the worst weather condition.
- The Appalachian Mountains are the most beautiful mountains in the U.S.
- Ice cream tastes better than any other dessert.
- More people visit Mount Rushmore during the summer than during any other season.
- In 2001 we had fourteen inches of rain.
- Kids should read at least 30 books a year.
- Elephants are the largest animals in the world.
- More children in our town play on a baseball team than on any other sports team.

Fact-and-Opinion Bingo Card 1

Opinion about mountains	Fact about an animal	Opinion about a book	Opinion about weather
Fact about a sport	Fact about a state	Fact about mountains	Fact about a season
Fact about a book	Fact about the weather	Opinion about an animal	Fact about a food item
Opinion about a sport	Opinion about a state	Opinion about a food item	Opinion about a season

Fact-and-Opinion Bingo Card 2

Fact about the weather	Fact about an animal	Fact about a sport	Opinion about mountains
Opinion about weather	Fact about a state	Opinion about a book	Fact about a food item
Opinion about a season	Opinion about an animal	Opinion about a sport	Fact about a season
Fact about mountains	Opinion about a state	Opinion about a food item	Fact about a book

Fact-and-Opinion Bingo Card 3

Fact about the weather	Fact about an animal	Opinion about a sport	Opinion about weather
Fact about a sport	Fact about a state	Fact about mountains	Fact about a season
Opinion about a season	Opinion about an animal	Opinion about a book	Fact about a food item
Opinion about mountains	Opinion about a state	Opinion about a food item	Fact about a book

Fact-and-Opinion Bingo Card 4

Fact about a state	Fact about an animal	Opinion about a food item	Opinion about a season
Fact about the weather	Opinion about a state	Opinion about weather	Opinion about a sport
Fact about mountains	Opinion about an animal	Opinion about a book	Fact about a food item
Opinion about mountains	Fact about a book	Fact about a sport	Fact about a season

Fact-and-Opinion Bingo Card 5

Fact about a sport	Fact about an animal	Fact about mountains	Fact about a food item
Fact about the weather	Fact about a book	Opinion about a book	Fact about a state
Fact about a season	Opinion about an animal	Opinion about weather	Opinion about a season
Opinion about mountains	Opinion about a food item	Opinion about a sport	Opinion about a state

Fact-and-Opinion Bingo Card 6

Fact about a food item	Fact about an animal	Fact about a state	Opinion about weather
Fact about a sport	Fact about mountains	Opinion about a sport	Fact about a season
Opinion about a season	Fact about the weather	Opinion about a book	Opinion about mountains
Opinion about a state	Opinion about an animal	Opinion about a food item	Fact about a book

Mini-Lesson #24: Main Idea

Teacher Lesson Plan

Objective

Students will identify the *main idea* and *supporting details* of two paragraphs.

Summary

In this mini-lesson the teacher will lead students in a discussion of what a *main idea* is and what supporting details are. The teacher and students will look at an example paragraph and identify the main idea and supporting details together. Then students will read a paragraph on their own and identify the main idea and supporting details.

Materials

- overhead transparency or copies of "Tiger" (page 73)
- "Road Trips" student activity sheet (1 copy per student, page 74)

Time: 20 minutes

Lesson

1. Introduction: Ask students what the *main idea* of a piece of writing is. Lead students to understand that the main idea of a piece of writing is what the author's main point is. If the author could summarize his or her writing in one or two sentences, that would be the main idea of the writing.

2. Tell students that authors use examples and descriptions to prove or better explain their main idea. Explain that we call these examples and descriptions *supporting details*.

3. Display overhead or distribute copies of "Tiger." Read the directions and the paragraph about Tiger together with the students. Direct students to identify the main idea of the paragraph and write it on the graphic organizer. (*Tiger was a funny cat.*) Remind students that authors support and further explain their main idea with descriptions or examples. Remind students that we call these *supporting details*. Lead students to identify two supporting details and write them on the graphic organizer. (*Tiger drank from the fish aquarium. Tiger drank from the dog's bath water.*)

4. Explain to students that they will now read a paragraph and complete a graphic organizer on their own. Distribute "Road Trips" student activity sheets and review directions with students. Allow students time to work independently. *See answer key below.*

Silent Reading Practice

Refer to pages 88 and 89 for corresponding reproducible student sheets and directions.

Answer Key (page 74)

Main idea: To have a successful road trip, you must make proper traveling plans.

Possible supporting details: Decide where you want to go and how long you want to be gone. Plan your route on a map. Locate hotels, campgrounds, or friends' and relatives' homes for overnight stays. Call ahead and make reservations for where you will stay.

Name_____   **Date** _____

Tiger

Directions: Read the following paragraph. Then identify the main idea and write two supporting details. Write them in the graphic organizer below.

Tiger was the funniest cat we have ever had. He was the first cat to start drinking from our fish aquarium. I would laugh so hard every time I saw Tiger perched up on the fish aquarium, lapping up water from the water filter system! He never bothered the fish; he just loved to drink their water! Another funny thing that Tiger did was drink from the dog's bath water. Whenever we would be giving the dog a bath, Tiger would waltz over and start lapping up water from the tub. I don't think the dog appreciated that, but we sure thought it was funny! Tiger was definitely a very funny cat.

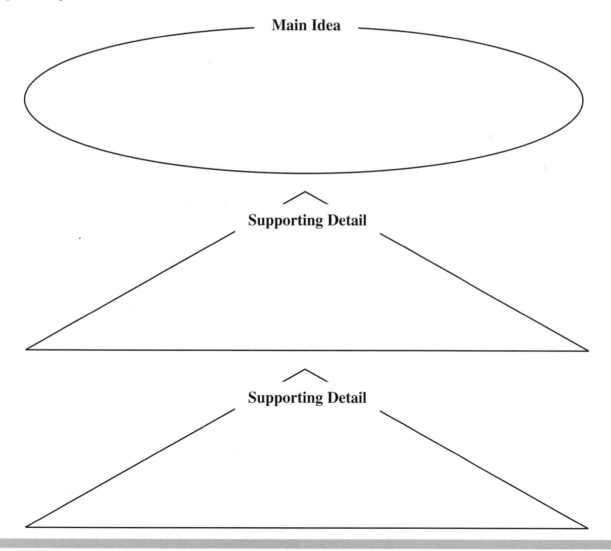

Main Idea

Supporting Detail

Supporting Detail

Name_____ **Date**_____

Road Trips

Directions: Read the following paragraph. Then identify the main idea and write two supporting details. Write them in the graphic organizer below.

To have a successful road trip, you must make proper traveling plans. First, you should decide where you want to go and how long you want your trip to be. Next, you must plan your traveling route on a map. You may even want to check your route on several maps to make sure that you have chosen the best plan. Thirdly, you must locate hotels, camping grounds, or relatives' and friends' homes where you will stay. It is always a good idea to call and make reservations ahead of time. Finally, you are ready to pack your belongings, jump in the car, and sit back and enjoy your vacation!

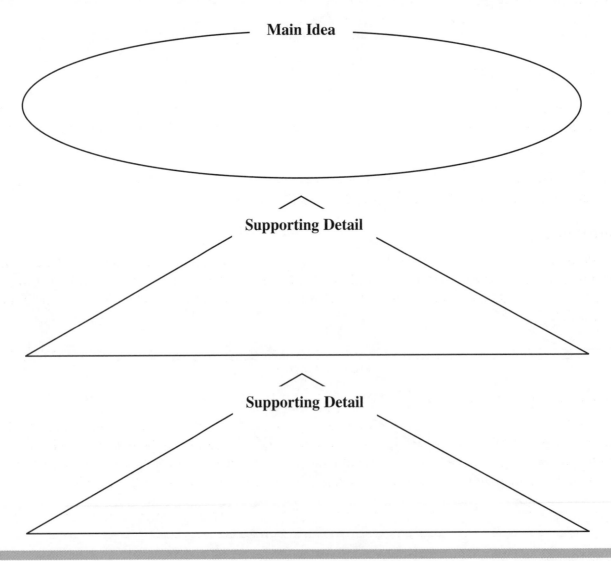

Main Idea

Supporting Detail

Supporting Detail

Teacher Lesson Plan

Objective

Students will identify the *main idea* and *supporting details* of a nonfiction article.

Summary

In this mini-lesson the teacher will lead students in a review of what a *main idea* is and what *supporting details* are. Then the students will read a one-page informational article and complete a graphic organizer with the main idea and supporting details of the article.

Materials

- "One Man of Peace" student activity sheets (1 copy per student, pages 76, 77)

Time: 20 minutes

Lesson

1. Introduction: Ask students what a main idea is and what supporting details are. Ask students why authors use supporting details in their writing. (*Authors use supporting details to prove or better explain their main idea.*) Ask students what a piece of writing would be like if it did not have a main idea. (*It would be confusing and would be difficult to understand because it would not have one main point or a clear focus.*)

2. Remind students of how they identified the main idea and supporting details of paragraphs in the previous lesson. Tell students that today they will read a longer writing selection and complete a similar graphic organizer to show the main idea and supporting details of the selection.

3. Distribute "One Man of Peace" student activity sheets and review directions together. Allow students time to work independently. *See answer key below.*

More Practice

For additional practice, select articles from a local newspaper and clip the titles from the articles. Have students match each article to its corresponding title, or have students create their own titles for the articles. Discuss with students how the titles of articles oftentimes give you a hint about the main idea of the article.

Answer Key (page 77)

Main Idea: Gandhi was a peaceful man.

Possible supporting Details: Although Gandhi was arrested and attacked, he did not speak angrily or cause harm to those people who were against him. Gandhi peacefully helped the people of India protest against the unjust laws. Gandhi taught people that they must be peaceful and return love for hate. Gandhi was a peaceful leader, helping India get its freedom from Britain.

Name _____   **Date** _____

One Man of Peace

Mahatma Gandhi has inspired many important leaders of the world. Gandhi led a life of peaceful resistance to unjust policies. Although he was often attacked and imprisoned for his ideas and acts, Gandhi refused to speak angrily against, or cause harm to, those who hurt him. Many important leaders use Gandhi's life as an example of how to help people and peacefully stand up for one's rights.

In 1893 Gandhi went to South Africa and peacefully helped the people win new laws. When Gandhi saw how unfair the people of darker skin—including Indians—were treated in South Africa, Gandhi decided to work for new laws. Gandhi peacefully set about showing that South Africa needed to change. Although Gandhi was a respected, educated man, he stopped wearing his fancy clothes and committed to wearing only a loincloth and shawl—the clothes of peasants in India. People joined Gandhi in his effort to win new laws, and eventually, after much resistance, they were able to win new laws for South Africa.

In 1915 Gandhi returned to India and became a peaceful leader in the movement to free India from British rule. Gandhi also worked to help the many poor people of India. As he did in South Africa, Gandhi taught the people that they must be brave and that they must return love for hate. After much resistance, India won its independence in 1947.

Gandhi's peaceful, powerful way of helping people and leading people to stand up for their rights has influenced many recent leaders. Martin Luther King, Jr. in the United States, Ella Bhatt in India, and Marina Silva in Brazil are only a few of the life-changing leaders who have noted Gandhi as an important influence in their lives. Gandhi's life shows us all that we can accomplish great tasks in peaceful ways.

One Man of Peace *(cont.)*

Directions: Carefully read "One Man of Peace." Then complete the chart below. Write the main idea of "One Man of Peace" in the oval and then write three supporting details in the triangles below.

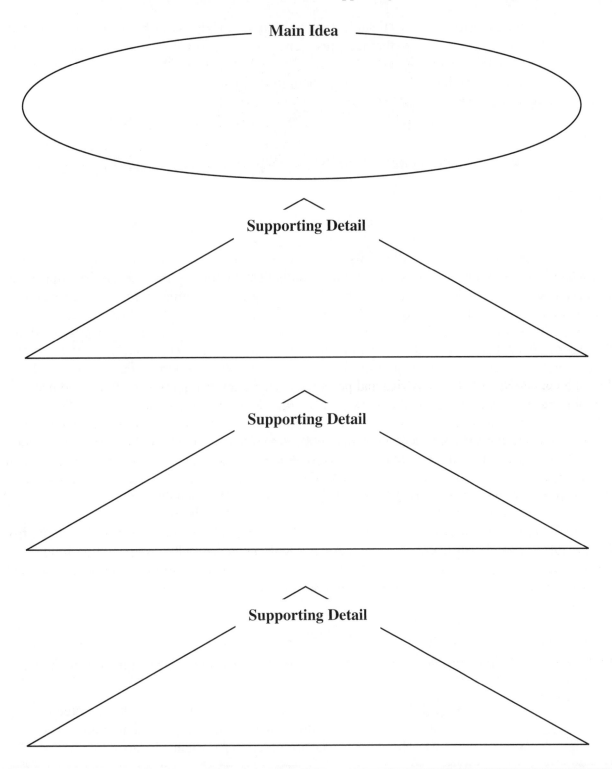

Main Idea

Supporting Detail

Supporting Detail

Supporting Detail

Mini-Lesson #26: Main Idea

Teacher Lesson Plan

Objective

Students will identify the main idea and supporting details of a short story.

Summary

In this mini-lesson, the teacher will lead students in a discussion about supporting details. The students will complete a student activity sheet that requires them to read a short story and complete a graphic organizer with the main idea and supporting details of the story. Finally, the teacher will review the student activity sheets with the students and help them to understand that not all details in a piece of writing are supporting details.

Materials

- "The Store Manager" student activity sheets (1 copy per student, pages 79, 80)

Time: 20 minutes

Lesson

1. Introduction: Ask students if all details in a piece of writing are supporting details. Discuss with students how supporting details are only the details that support the main idea. Sometimes authors give you details to better understand something in the writing, but those details do not necessarily support the main idea of the writing.

2. Explain to students that today they will read the short story "The Store Manager" and complete a graphic organizer that asks them to identify the *main* idea and supporting details. Remind students that not all details are supporting details. Explain to students that after they have completed the activity, you will discuss their work.

3. Distribute "The Store Manager" student activity sheets and review directions together. Allow students time to work independently. *See answer key below.*

4. When students are finished, review the answers together. Ask students to underline or highlight the sentences that gave the main idea and supporting details in the story. Ask students to identify some details from the story that were not supporting details. (*e.g., Mr. Humphrey's Uncle Ben was the store manager of a shoe store.*) Ask students to explain why these details were not supporting details. Explain to students that although these details are important in the story, they do not support the main idea in the way that the supporting details do.

Answer Key (page 80)

Main Idea: Mr. Humphreys is an excellent store manager because he has had many experiences working at stores.

Supporting Details: As a child, Mr. Humphreys swept the floor of his uncle's shoe store. As a teenager, he worked as a stock boy at a grocery store. After graduating, Mr. Humphreys became a clerk at a department store. Mr. Humphreys was promoted to Assistant Manager.

Name_____   **Date** _____

Directions: Read "The Store Manager" below. Then complete the graphic organizer on page 80 with the main idea and supporting details. Write the main idea in the middle oval and the supporting details in the surrounding ovals.

The Store Manager

Mr. Humphreys is an excellent store manager because he has had many experiences of working at stores. When Mr. Humphreys was a young boy, he helped his Uncle Ben by sweeping the floor of his small shoe store. Uncle Ben was the store manager, and he would spend hours telling Mr. Humphreys stories about how to be a successful store manager. Mr. Humphreys was always intrigued by his uncle's stories and decided that he wanted to become a store manager himself one day.

When Mr. Humphreys became a teenager, he began working as a stock boy at the local grocery store. He often worked long hours on weekends, and he learned a lot about how stores are run. He would talk with all of the workers at the grocery store to learn exactly what they had to do as a part of their job.

After graduating from school, Mr. Humphreys began working as a clerk at a large department store downtown. Mr. Humphreys was always trying to become just a little bit better at what he did. His boss noticed how hard Mr. Humphreys was working and promoted him to an assistant manager position. Mr. Humphreys was very excited, and he began to work even harder. Several years later, the store needed a new full-time store manager. Mr. Humphreys nervously applied for the position, and he was immediately promoted. Mr. Humphreys was very happy that he had finally fulfilled his dream of becoming a store manager.

Name _____   **Date** _____

The Store Manager

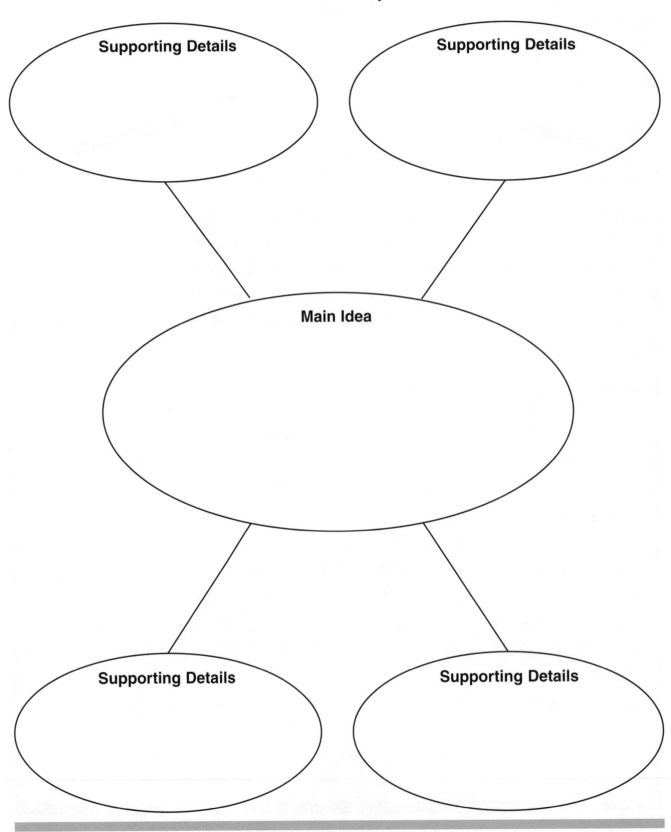

Supporting Details

Supporting Details

Main Idea

Supporting Details

Supporting Details

Silent Reading Practice: Context Clues

Directions: As you read silently, look for unknown words. Use context clues to figure out the meaning of those words. Complete the activity below.

Title of Book _____

Author _____

Unknown word _____ Page number _____

Copy the sentence in your book that contains the word:

_____

_____

_____

Using context clues, write a definition for the word:

_____

_____

Now look up your word in the dictionary and write the dictionary definition:

_____

_____

Correct your context clues definition if necessary, or rewrite the dictionary definition in your own words:

_____

_____

Name_____

Date _____

Silent Reading Practice: Sequence

Directions: As you read silently, write down events as they are mentioned in the book. Write down the page number where each event can be found. Put a star (☆) beside events that are flashbacks.

Title of Book _____

Author _____

Event #1—Page ___

Event #2—Page ___

Event #3—Page ___

Event #4—Page ___

Name_____

Date _____

Silent Reading Practice: Setting

Directions: As you read silently, look for details that the author gives you about the setting of the story. Complete the activity below.

Title of Book _____

Author _____

Sentences and phrases that the author uses to describe the setting:

- Page # ___ _____

    _____

    _____

- Page # ___ _____

    _____

    _____

- Page # ___ _____

    _____

    _____

- Page # ___ _____

    _____

    _____

Using the details above, draw the setting of your story below.

Name_____   **Date** _____

Silent Reading Practice: Cause and Effect

Directions: As you read silently, look for cause-and-effect events. Complete the chart below.

Title of Book _____

Author _____

Cause Event #1:

_____

_____

_____

Page number _____

Effect Event #1:

_____

_____

_____

Page number _____

Cause Event #2:

_____

_____

_____

Page number _____

Effect Event #2:

_____

_____

_____

Page number _____

Name _____   **Date** _____

Silent Reading Practice: Prediction

Directions: As you read silently, record your predictions in the chart below.

Title of Book _____

Author _____

Page #	What is happening in the story . . .	What I predict will happen next . . .

Name_____   **Date** _____

Silent Reading Practice: Inference

Directions: As you read silently, think about what inferences you are able to make. Remember that inferences are conclusions that you are able to make about the clues or facts given in a story. Complete the chart below.

Title of Book _____

Author _____

Inference #1
With the following clues and facts from the story: (page _____)
_____
_____
_____
_____
I infer that . . .
_____
_____
_____

Inference #2
With the following clues and facts from the story: (page _____)
_____
_____
_____
_____
I infer that . . .
_____
_____
_____

Name _____ **Date** _____

Silent Reading Practice: Fact and Opinion

Directions: As you read silently, look for facts and opinions that are mentioned in your book. Record them in the chart below.

Title of Book _____

Author _____

F A C T S	Fact_____ _____ Page # _____
	Fact_____ _____ Page # _____

O P I N I O N S	Opinion_____ _____ Page # _____
	Opinion_____ _____ Page # _____

Name_____   **Date**_____

Silent Reading Practice: Main Idea (Book)

Directions: As you read silently, think about the main idea and supporting details of your book. Complete the information below.

Title of Book _____

Author _____

Main Idea

_____

_____

Supporting Details

Page _____ _____

_____

_____

Page _____ _____

_____

_____

Page _____ _____

_____

Page _____ _____

_____

_____

Name_____ **Date** _____

Silent Reading Practice: Main Idea (Article)

Directions: As you read silently, think about what the main idea of your article is. Write the main idea of your article in the center shape. Write the supporting details in the surrounding ovals.

Title of Article _____

Author _____

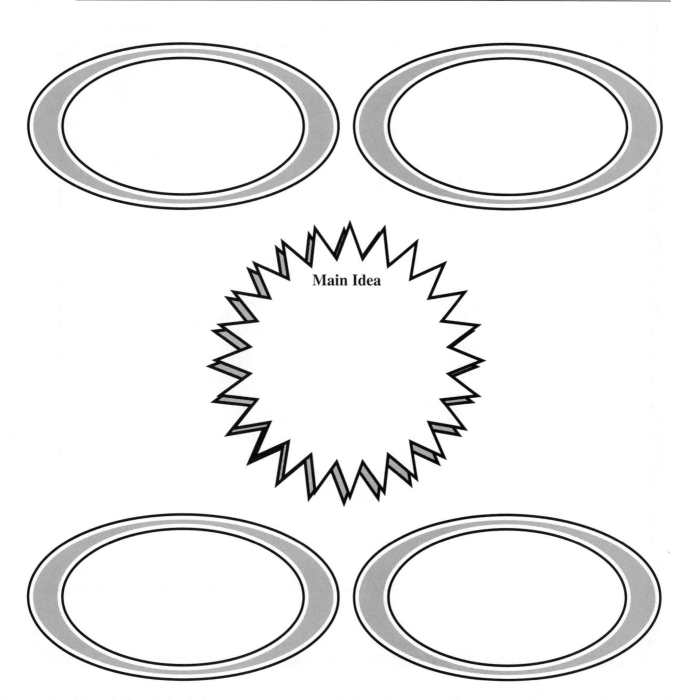

Literature Connections

Setting

When I Was Young in the Mountains by Cynthia Rylant (Dutton, 1982)

Review the two main parts of a setting ("when" and "where"). Read *When I Was Young in the Mountains* by Cynthia Rylant with the class and tell students to pay special attention to the setting of the story. Use "When I was Young in the Mountains" student activity sheet (page 91) to help students reflect on the setting.

Setting

Peppe the Lamplighter by Elisa Bartone (Lothrup, Lee, Shepard; 1993)

Review how a setting can affect the mood of a story. Discuss how authors usually give you an idea of the setting at the beginning of the story. Tell students that you will only read them the beginning of *Peppe the Lamplighter* today and then ask them to complete "Peppe's Setting" student activity sheet (page 92). (*Note: You can use the entire story of* Peppe the Lamplighter *in the Prediction Literature Connection below.*)

Prediction

Peppe the Lamplighter by Elisa Bartone (Lothrup, Lee, Shepard; 1993)

Review the importance of using information from the story to make predictions. Read *Peppe the Lamplighter* by Elisa Bartone to the class and pause periodically for students to make predictions. Guide students to use the "Peppe Predictions" student activity sheet (page 93) to record their predictions. Discuss students' predictions and reasons for their predictions.

Prediction

Two Bad Ants by Chris Van Allsburg (Houghton, Mifflin, 1997)

Review the importance of using specific clues from a story to make your predictions. Explain that in *Two Bad Ants* Christ Van Allsburg gives many clues to help his readers make predictions. Explain to students the directions for "Where Are Those Two Bad Ants?" student activity sheet (page 94) and guide them to complete the activity as you read *Two Bad Ants*.

Inference

Window by Jeannie Baker (Greenwillow Books, 1991)

Review the meaning of "inference" and the importance of making inferences while reading. Discuss with students the difference between an observation and an inference. Explain to students that *Window* has no words, but it does tell a story. Tell students that they will need to make inferences about what story the author is telling. Read *Window* by Jeannie Baker and have students complete the "Window Inferences" student activity sheet (page 95) to record both their observations and inferences.

Inference

Yo! Yes? by Chris Raschka (Orchard Books, 1993)

Review with students that good readers use clues to develop conclusions, or inferences, while reading. Remind students that making inferences is somewhat like "reading between the lines" or figuring out the story that is not directly told. Explain to students that *Yo! Yes?* has very few words, and so they must use clues to develop good inferences about what is happening in the story. Read *Yo! Yes?* by Chris Raschka with your class and guide students to complete "Yes, More Inference Practice" student activity sheet (page 96).

Name_____   **Date**_____

When I Was Young in the Mountains

Directions: As you read *When I Was Young in the Mountains*, think about the setting of the story. Complete the questions below.

1. What is the setting of *When I Was Young in the Mountains?*

   _____

   _____

2. In the boxes below, write or draw about two specific details that Cynthia Rylant uses to tell readers more about the setting of the story.

Name _____   **Date** _____

Peppe's Setting

Directions: After listening to the beginning of *Peppe the Lamplighter*, answer the questions below.

1. What is the setting of *Peppe the Lamplighter*?

    _____

    _____

2. What is the mood of the story so far? How does the setting help set the mood?

    _____

    _____

3. Use the chart below to compare and contrast Peppe's setting with your own.

    _____

    _____

The Setting of Peppe's Life	The Setting of My Life

Name_____ **Date** _____

Peppe Predictions

Directions: As you read *Peppe the Lamplighter*, use the chart below to record your predictions about what will happen next in the story.

Predictions About Peppe the Lamplighter	Observations and Experiences That Helped Me Make My Predictions

Name_____   **Date** _____

Where Are Those Two Bad Ants?

Directions: As you read *Two Bad Ants*, complete the chart below. In the box on the left, write clues that the author gives you about where the two bad ants are, and then in the box on the right, write where you think the ants are.

Clues About Where the Ants Are	Where I Think They Are

Window Inferences

Directions: Complete the following chart during and after reading *Window*.

My Notes of Facts and Observations from *Window*

After considering all of the facts, make some inferences about *Window*. (What story is this book telling? What is the author's message? What is the cause of the changes in the story?)

_____

_____

_____

_____

_____

_____

_____

Yes, More Inference Practice

Directions: After reading *Yo! Yes?* complete the questions below.

1. *Yo! Yes?* has very few words, but the book does tell a story. Using inferences, what would you say the story of *Yo! Yes?* is?

_____

_____

_____

_____

_____

_____

_____

2. Choose one picture from *Yo! Yes?* If you could add more words to the page, what would you add?

_____

_____

_____

_____

_____

_____

_____